Getting Up Again and Other Stories We Tell Ourselves About Being Strong

Herman Veitch

Published by Herman Veitch, 2024.

While every precaution has been taken in the preparation of this book, the publisher assumes no responsibility for errors or omissions, or for damages resulting from the use of the information contained herein.

GETTING UP AGAIN AND OTHER STORIES WE TELL OURSELVES ABOUT BEING STRONG

First edition. August 5, 2024.

ISBN: 979-8224549061

Written by Herman Veitch.

Table of Contents

Contributors

Thank you, to the following people on whom I leaned heavily:

- Dorian Haarhoff for his writing coaching.
- Anne Haarhoff for her proofreading.
- Alison Dyson for the book cover photo. You can find her at https://www.alisadysonphotography.com/
- Hetsie Veitch for her gift of taking care of the detail making this book 80% better.
- Friends, family, and clients that informed my ideas.
- So many other authors who have shaped my thinking and perspective on life. I tried to give references as much as possible, but I am sure I missed some. Sorry. Please let me know.

Most of the graphics in the text were sourced from https://pixabay.com/

Getting up Again

And other stories we tell ourselves about being strong

Introduction

"Do not judge me by my successes, judge me by how many times I fell down and got back up again." (Nelson Mandela)

In a coastal village nestled between rolling hills and the rhythmic whispers of the sea, a young fisherman named Liam faced a tempest that transcended the realm of mere weather. The serenity of his coastal home belied the storm that had torn apart his family one fateful night, claiming his father and other men in the village, leaving behind a void in the community as vast as the horizon.

While the mourning clouds refused to part, Liam, with a heavy heart, repaired an old boat, forgotten by the storm, and set out to sea. Each dawn saw him facing the tumultuous ocean, his eyes reflecting determination and the echoes of his father's laughter, lost to the abyss. The skeptical whispers of the villagers couldn't drown Liam's resolve. With each repaired net and restored sail, he not only mended his boat but stitched together the torn fabric of his soul. His sea-bound odyssey became a dance with despair and hope.

Days blurred into nights, storms roared, yet Liam persisted. Over time, the muted colours of the village were rekindled with the hues of restored hope, and his battered boat, now a symbol of loss and redemption, sailed back not just with a hold full of fish but also with the intangible treasures of endurance and healing.

The village, once cloaked in grief, transformed into a tapestry woven with threads of shared struggle and triumphant resilience. In Liam's story, the people discovered not just a fisherman but a living testament to the strength that arises from the depths of despair. The salty air now carried whispers of inspiration, echoing the resilience that, like Liam, had weathered the storms, and emerged bathed in the golden light of newfound strength.[i]

Liam's is a story of each of us overcoming the ups and downs the sea of life takes us through. In "*Getting Up Again: And Other Stories We Tell Ourselves About Being Strong*" I guide you as we explore how to live with resilience. Resilience refers to the ability of an individual, community, organisation or system to withstand, adapt to and recover from adversity, challenges or setbacks. It is the capacity to bounce back and learn from experiences. We maintain or regain a sense of well-being and functionality in the face of life's challenges.

Resilience involves the development of coping mechanisms, emotional strength, flexibility, and the ability to navigate and overcome obstacles. Here in the pages of *Getting Up Again* we explore the elements of building resilience. We look at how we can foster positive attitudes, social support networks and effective problem-solving skills to enhance our ability to cope with adversity and thrive.

Without resilience, individuals tend to deal with increased stress and mental health issues. A reduced ability to cope with setbacks leads to lower life satisfaction and vulnerability to illnesses. This strains our relationships, hinders problem-solving, and isolates us. The absence of resilience also contributes to reduced productivity in communities, affecting their ability to recover from crises and adapt to change.

Research on the role resilience plays in people's lives shows that there are teachable skills that enable people to be more resilient.[ii] This book introduces some of these skills. Just like exercise enhances our physical health, practising resilience enhances our emotional health.

These skills are meant to achieve a variety of goals such as overcoming childhood obstacles, navigating your way through adversities, bouncing back after setbacks, and reaching out to broaden your experience of the world. In essence, they enable us to solve problems, take appropriate risks, and accurately forecast the implications of adversity. These skills also provide a remarkable opportunity to look inward, to get to know ourselves – really know ourselves – and to connect deeply with others.

This book offers a resilience pyramid. The building blocks are based on the research of Carol Ryff and her colleagues.[iii] They identified six dimensions that build up psychological well-being, namely: Positive Self-Esteem, Autonomy, Positive Relationships, Environmental Mastery, Personal Growth and Living with Purpose. Of these six, I take the first four and break them down into easily understandable and applicable concepts.

The foundational building blocks of our pyramid are self-esteem and autonomy. We explore the stories we tell ourselves about who we are, and with whose authority we are who we are. The next layer of the pyramid is essential to our well-being. We dedicate this layer to cultivating positive relationships with others. The tip of the pyramid is mastering our environment. Everything builds up to this, as we grow our resilience through our interaction with our environment. As in Liam's story, we will catch no fish if we do not set out to sea.

My wish for you in reading this book is that, in the end, you will not only survive the storms but thrive because of them.

"It's about being able to go through the grind, willing to get back up when you're knocked down. And when life's not going well, not getting down on yourself and just getting back up and getting back to work and striving to be the best you can be." (Robbie Lawler)

Part 1 – Positive Self-Esteem

Because one believes in oneself, one doesn't try to convince others. Because one is content with oneself, one doesn't need others' approval. Because one accepts oneself, the whole world accepts him or her." (Lao Tzu)

Chapter 1 - Our Stories

Embarking on a journey to cultivate internal strength begins with the cornerstone of positive self-esteem. We all hold an estimation of ourselves. Some of us overestimate while most underestimate. Few have a healthy self-estimation. In this chapter, we start to build our healthy self-esteem.

"Estimation of ourselves" refers to the subjective evaluation or judgement we make about our worth as individuals. We form perceptions and beliefs about our competencies, character and significance in various aspects of life, including personal, social and professional domains. Positive self-esteem reflects a favourable estimation, while negative self-esteem suggests a less favourable or even critical evaluation of one's worth and capabilities. This internal audit significantly influences our thoughts, emotions and behaviours, shaping our overall well-being and interactions with the world.

So, what does a healthy self-estimation look like? There are three building blocks. Persons with a healthy self-estimation have a positive attitude towards themselves, they acknowledge and accept multiple aspects of themselves, including desirable and less desirable qualities, and they feel positive about their past life. We will look at each one of these three building blocks in this and the next two chapters.

We start with exploring what it means to have a positive attitude towards oneself.

The stories we tell ourselves

As humans, we are constantly busy making sense of the world we live in. In this, we mirror what the rest of nature, of whom we are part, is doing. Taking the signals that our senses pick up from the environment to determine whether or not our environment is safe or dangerous, we instinctively assess if what is coming our way is rewarding or punishing.

All this happens at a biological foundational level. The way we make sense of these signals is to weave them together in a story that is logical to us. A story that we can repeat to explain triggers that affected our experience.

We see this clearly when small children tell us what happened in the playgroup. We tell our friends the stories of what happened to us at work, our news outlets tell us stories of what is happening all over the world, and our movies and TV series tell us entertaining stories.

The point is clear. Storytelling is at the essence of sense-making. This is especially true when we look at our self-estimation. The stories we tell ourselves about ourselves determine if we feel good or bad about ourselves.

We can identify these stories by listening to our internal dialogue or observing ourselves telling our friends or family. As we listen to these stories, we will start to notice a pattern. Story themes reappear often, and we can start labelling these themes. An example of a common theme is the 'imposter syndrome' or the 'I am not good enough' theme song. A learned professor friend once confided, "I'm scared that if my colleagues found out how little I know, they would ridicule me." This self-doubt comes from a brilliant person whose groundbreaking research changed the direction of her field. Yet, she felt like a fraud. Despite her accolades, she battled the imposter syndrome-themed story, as she believed she didn't truly belong.

These themes become scripts that we follow unconsciously. It works like an operating system that runs in the background. All other software runs on it in the foreground.

Some authors call these operating systems paradigms, mental models, worldviews, or belief systems. I like the term belief systems because it captures how these scripts, running in the background, are how we believe the world is supposed to be. Because there is more than one script running simultaneously, they form a system that influences each belief and each other. Therefore, belief systems are the goggles we look through to see and make sense of the world.

So, how is this relevant to us, trying to understand how to embrace resilience and vitality?

Marc of marcandangel.com shares the following story:[iv]

"She rarely makes eye contact. Instead, she looks down at the ground. The ground is safer. Because, unlike people, it expects nothing in return. The ground accepts her for who she is right now.

As she sits at the bar next to me, she stares down at her vodka tonic, and then the ground, and then her vodka tonic. "Most people don't get me," she says. "They ask me questions like, 'What's your problem?' or 'Were you beaten as a child?' But I never respond. Because I don't feel like explaining myself, and I don't think they care anyway."

Just then, a young man sits down at the bar on the opposite side of her. He's a little drunk, and says, "You're pretty. May I buy you a drink?" She stays silent and looks back down at the ground. After an awkward moment, he accepts the rejection, gets up, and walks away.

"Would you prefer that I leave too?" I ask. "No," she says without glancing upward. "But I could use some fresh air. You don't have to come, but you can if you want to." I followed her outside and we sat on a street curb in front of the bar.

"Brrr... it's a really chilly night!"

"Tell me about it," she says while maintaining her usual downward gaze. The warm vapor from her breath cuts through the cold air and bounces off of the ground in front of her. "So why are you out here with me? I mean, wouldn't you rather be inside in the warmth, talking to normal people about normal things?"

"I'm out here because I want to be. Because I'm not normal. And look, I can see my breath, and we're in San Diego. That's not normal either. Oh, and you're wearing Airwalk sneakers, and so am I, which may have been normal in 1994, but not anymore."

She glances up at me and smiles, this time exhaling her breath upward into the moonlight. "I see you're wearing a ring. You're married, right?"

"Yeah," I reply. "My wife Angel is just getting off work now and heading here to meet me for dinner."

She nods her head and then looks back at the ground. "Well, you're off the market... and safe, I guess. So can I tell you a story?"

"I'm listening."

As she speaks, her emotional gaze shifts from the ground to my eyes, to the moonlit sky, to the ground, and back to my eyes again. This rotation continues in a loop for the duration of her story. And every time her eyes meet mine she holds them there for a few seconds longer than she did on the previous rotation.

I don't interject. I listen to every word. And I assimilate the raw emotion present in the tone of her voice and in the depth of her eyes.

When she finishes, she says, "Well, now you know my story. You think I'm a freak, don't you?"

"Place your right hand on your chest," I tell her. She does. "Do you feel something?" I ask.

"Yeah, I feel my heartbeat."

"Now close your eyes, place both your hands on your face, and move them around slowly." She does. "What do you feel now?" I ask.

"Well, I feel my eyes, my nose, my mouth... I feel my face."

"That's right," I reply. "But unlike you, stories don't have heartbeats, and they don't have faces. Because stories are not alive – they're not people. They're just stories.

She stares into my eyes for a prolonged moment, smiles sincerely, and says, "Just stories we live through."

"Yeah... And stories we learn from."

So, we choose which story to live by. The Psalmist says, "We spend our years as a tale *that is told*" (Psalm 90: v9). Yet, positive stories build us up. Negative ones break us down.

Our belief systems or the life stories we choose to tell either result in a positive or a negative attitude toward ourselves. If, for example, the story we tell ourselves is that we are not good enough, we will perceive ourselves accordingly. Our shoulders will hunch, and we present ourselves as someone who is of no importance.

The problem with this is that we may also have a story of a belief system that we are special and worthy of love. How can we solve this paradox?

In technical terms, this paradox is called cognitive dissonance. Cognitive dissonance describes the conflict between two belief systems. Allow me to explain. In the story we tell ourselves, most of us play the role of a good person. This is normal and healthy for our psychological well-being. Sometimes though, information comes to us that shows we are not as good as we thought we were. This could include an awareness of the consequences of our actions or feedback we receive from someone else.

One of two things tends to happen when we get this information. We either reject it or embrace it. Rejection happens in many forms. We ignore it, we deny it, or we project it onto someone or something else. When we embrace this information, we allow it to influence us. This influence can be either constructive or destructive. Destructive influence breaks down the healthy self-story and replaces it with an unhealthy story or belief system. This tends to spiral into the rest of our views about ourselves and how we show up in the world.

There is a different, more effective way. We can choose to make the influence constructive. When we choose the constructive way, we take the information and use it to grow and become better. The question now comes up, how exactly do we do this? To find this effective way, we look at how the brain works.

Uncovering the nuts and bolts of our mindset

The first thing to know about our brains is that, because it is so energy intensive (our brain is but 2% of our body mass, but uses 20% of our energy), it constantly seeks energy-efficient ways to work. As soon as it can, it creates a shortcut. All our habits, biases and preconceived ideas are such shortcuts. Anything we do automatically is a shortcut, from driving a car to scratching our heads. To snap judgements about someone. Our belief systems, which also fall into this category, are nothing more than well-established neurological connections.

The second thing to know about our brain is that it is constantly regenerating itself. Just like our skin constantly creates new skin cells, our brain constantly creates new neurons to renew itself. This is called brain plasticity. Neuroscience has disproved the old view that the brain stops developing at a certain age. Whenever we learn something new or gain new insight, new connections are made between billions of neurons.

When we combine neurological shortcuts and neuroplasticity, we arrive at a place where we can re-create our belief systems at will. How do we do this?

The psychologist Albert Ellis provides us with a useful tool. It is simply applying the ABC to our thinking. "A" stands for activating events, "B" for belief systems, and "C" for consequences.

Normally we believe that A (Activating Event) causes C (Consequence - How you feel about the event). But the truth is, C is caused by B (what you tell yourself about the event - our belief system) that interprets A.

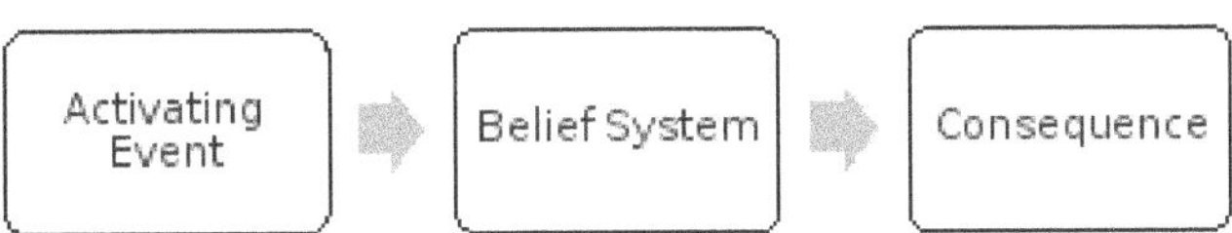

To illustrate this, we can use the insights of another great psychologist, Martin Seligman.[v] In his research, he identified learned helplessness as the opposite of resilience. Learned helplessness can be identified by three common scripts most of us use at some time or another. We make things *personal, permanent* or *pervasive* (the 3 Ps). Let's explore each to illustrate their impact.

Let's start with making things personal. Say you compliment me on the shirt I am wearing. Unbeknownst to you, I hate the shirt; it scratches my neck, and it was the last clean shirt I could wear. My response to your compliment is, "Pfff, don't be ridiculous." In response to my dismissive statement, you may think, "I am not going to say anything nice to this guy again. He is grumpy."

When we apply the ABC to this situation, the activating event was your compliment. The consequence was my dismissive response. The belief system that interpreted your compliment was my dislike of the shirt. B is all about how we choose to react. This is our greatest freedom. My choice of a dismissive response becomes your activating event, which is interpreted by your belief system. So, the spiral continues.

If I had a learned helplessness response of taking things personally, my belief system could sound something like this, "Obviously, this person is sarcastic. Isn't it obvious I hate this shirt?"

My dismissive response to your compliment has nothing to do with you. It has everything to do with my internal script. In his book *The Four Agreements*, Don Miguel Ruiz teaches us a powerful antidote to this script.[vi] He says, "Nothing anybody does or says is because of you." People do or say because of their internal mental processes.

As a rule of thumb, we should not take ourselves too seriously. The uncomfortable truth is that we do when we take things personally. When we think that anything any person says or does is aimed at us, our script assumes that we are the center of the universe. We are not. We are part of the universe, but not the center. So, I invite you, to please resign as the general manager of the universe. Nothing needs to be taken personally. And if you do, know that you did so by choice.

The next learned helplessness script: We tend to make things permanent. Behind this script is our need for stability. We expect that things may not or will not change. That if something changes, we will lose control. This loss of control creates anxiety. So, to manage this anxiety, we tend to think and speak in absolutes.

How do we do this? Become aware of words like "always" and "never" in your language or thoughts. As someone said, "Never say never. It's a long time." For example, "you never wash the dishes", or "you are always late". These words are absolute. The danger of overusing them is that people stop taking us seriously. And deep down, we also stop believing in ourselves. This is not the way to build high self-esteem.

A beggar once gave a depressed king a ring. Inscribed on the inside were the words, "This too will pass." Fortunately for us, change is the only constant. This constant change hides a hidden blessing. When things go badly, we can stick it out, because change is coming. Also, when things are going well, be present and grateful for the good times, because change is coming. So, check your belief systems and update them with "This too shall change." It's like the weather that changes constantly.

The last learned helplessness script: We allow things to be pervasive. Pervasiveness describes a particular trait or characteristic present in many different contexts. For instance, we might describe someone as having a pervasive sense of humour, meaning that they tend to find things amusing in a variety of situations and settings.

This is a tricky script to manage. It is good to know that everything relates to everything else. Yet, everything is independent on its own as well.

Pervasiveness becomes unhealthy when we allow the negative to spill over from one situation to another, without giving the new situation a fair chance to show its uniqueness. When we messed up in one area, we believe we will mess up again in another area. We over-generalize the negative. The other side of the coin is also true. We could over-generalize our successes. Believing that because I was successful in the previous situation, I will be successful in this new situation as well. There is an ocean of difference between "I have failed at this" and "I am a failure."

I am sure you have made the connection already. I want to make it obvious. For us to be resilient the first building block is self-esteem built on stories or belief systems that validate our value.

If some of our stories do not add value, we can change them with the use of this ABC tool.

Wrap up

I want to press pause at this point. Let's reflect for a few moments on what was shared up to now.

In this chapter, we focused on cultivating a positive attitude toward ourselves. The stories we tell ourselves create our belief systems of how the world is supposed to be. These story scripts dictate how we interpret what happens to us. We choose these stories.

We then touched on two neurological facts. Our brains create shortcuts. Our brain constantly renews itself. Based on these facts we chose to re-write our ineffective mental scripts.

To re-write any script, we need to know what the current script is. To identify the current script, we introduced the ABC tool for observing our thoughts. We then applied this tool to three learned helplessness scripts, taking things personally, making them permanent, and allowing things to be pervasive.

In the process of rewriting the script we have about ourselves, it helps to know we are not the only ones doing it. And we can learn from those who share their new scripts.

In the next chapter, we look at how to acknowledge and accept multiple aspects of ourselves, but first I leave you with this poem by Rupi Kaur that demonstrates a rewritten script:[vii]

15

I Am Complete Simply Because I Am Imperfect.

we think we are lost
while our fuller
found and complete selves
are somewhere in the future
we get on our hands and knees
thinking self-improvement will
help us reach them
but this finding ourselves bullshit
is never going to end
i'm tired of putting off living until
i have more information on who i am
i'm a new person every month
always becoming and unbecoming
only to become again
our fuller selves are not off in the future
they're right here
in the only moment that exists
i don't need fixing
i will be searching for answers my whole life
not because i'm a half-formed thing
but because i'm brilliant enough to keep growing
everything necessary to live a vivid life
already exists in me

Chapter 2 – Celebrating Yourself

Introduction

In our story, Liam's sister Mia deals with the loss of their father in a different way. Preparing meals for the family became a meditation for her. Mia's recipe called for a blend of diverse flavours – sweet and savoury, bitter and spicy. Mia likened it to the blend of her own qualities. The sweetness of her kindness, the bitterness of her mistakes, the savoury moments of success, and the spicy challenges that added zest to her life.

As she diced onions, tears welled in her eyes, reminding her of the moments of vulnerability that made her human. Yet, she knew those tears would eventually enhance the overall flavour, just as acknowledging her weaknesses contributed to her personal growth.

As the dish simmered, Mia understood that life, like cooking, required balance. Accepting the imperfect mix of ingredients made the final creation uniquely hers. With a taste of her creation, Mia savoured the richness of self-acceptance, realizing that embracing both the good and bad within herself was the key to a fulfilling life, much like savouring the intricate flavours of a well-prepared meal.

Figure 1- Image by cromaconceptovisual from Pixabay

Mia's meditation resonates with me. I love food. And I am lucky enough to have a wife who loves cooking. You will easily come to the same conclusion when you look at me from the side. My side profile looks like half an avocado with its pit still in it, standing on two legs.

I love the aroma, texture and taste of explosions that come from each bite. When I eat an orange, I cup it in my hands to smell the peel before I peel it. Then I float away in the sweet juicy bite.

In this chapter, we focus on the celebration of your diversity just as we celebrate a sumptuous meal. We do this by accepting your talents and limitations as part of your self-esteem script. First, we make sure we have the right measuring equipment to measure the ingredients of ourselves. And then we explore the different spices that make up who we are – our personality traits.

Comparison and correct measurement

In societies there are hierarchies. This has been so since we started living together as human beings, which is basically from the start of our history. Today, we distinguish between formal hierarchies, like those in an organisation or the military, and the less obvious informal hierarchies that we find in our wider society.

In an informal social hierarchy, some people have more power and status than others, even if it's not something that is officially recognised or enforced. These hierarchies can be based on factors such as popularity, wealth, influence, and social skills. For example, people higher up in the hierarchy have more say in what games are played or who gets invited to events.

This hierarchical ladder is a natural occurrence, and we all stand on one of the rungs. Unfortunately, it is also open to abuse or misuse. In our teenage years, finding our place on this ladder is a normal aspect of psychological development. This goes on into our twenties and early thirties. Somewhere in this time frame, our identity stabilizes and is supposed to no longer be an issue, but it seems to be a lingering developmental phase for many people.

Let us explore how to move on with our lives.

Inherent in finding our place on the social hierarchy ladder is the process of comparison. Yes, we all automatically compare ourselves with those around us. The advice to not compare is a waste of words. What we need to do is to update and re-write the comparison software. This is just another way of saying we need to check the stories we tell ourselves about comparing ourselves with others.

Depending on the way we were raised and our life experiences, there can be bugs in our comparison software. One of the big and obvious bugs is to compare ourselves to the image social media portrays of the people we know. Knowing that this image is one-sided helps us debug our perception. People mostly post only their highlights on social media. The lowlights are kept private. Comparing your whole life with others' highlights is an unfair comparison.

This insight leads to an important point. We need to use the correct measurement when we compare. We do not measure distance with a thermometer, we measure temperature. In the same way, we must use the right measurement for ourselves.

What would a correct measurement be?

Instead of comparing ourselves to other peoples' projected social image, try focusing on our own progress and growth. Being better than our old self.

Another way to measure ourselves is to reflect on our values and priorities. What is important to us? What are our core beliefs? By aligning our actions and decisions with our values, we can create a sense of purpose and fulfilment. That said, there is no one "correct" way to measure ourselves. It's up to each one of us to decide what is important and meaningful and to set our own standards for success and happiness.

So, let me ask. What is important to you? What are your core beliefs about yourself? Do you see how you circle back to the stories you tell yourself about yourself?

A personality assessment offers a common tool to introduce us to our self-told stories.

Personality traits

Personality traits are the different ways we think, feel and act that make us unique individuals. They're like puzzle pieces that fit together to create our overall personality.

There are many different personality traits, like being outgoing or shy, being organised or messy, or being curious or cautious. Some people might have more of certain traits than others, which is what makes us all different.

Personality traits can be helpful because they can help us understand ourselves and others better. For example, if you're organised, you might be good at keeping your room clean or your work in order. Or if you're outgoing, you might be good at making new friends.

However, personality traits also have limitations. They don't tell us everything about a person, and they don't predict everything a person might do. For example, just because someone is outgoing doesn't mean they're always happy or confident.

Also, personality traits can change over time. So just because you might be shy now, does not mean you'll always be shy. You might become more outgoing as you grow and experience new things.

Personality assessments can be a useful tool for gaining self-awareness and understanding ourselves better. They can provide insights into our preferred communication style, work environment, and ways of thinking. In that sense, personality assessments can help us tell a more accurate and nuanced story about ourselves. By understanding our personality traits, we can gain insight into why we behave the way we do and how we can make the most of our talents while managing our limitations.

It's important to remember that personality assessments are just one tool for self-discovery, and they should not be used as a definitive measure of who we are. Our personality is influenced by many factors, including our experiences, values and beliefs.

It's also important to be mindful of how we interpret and use the results of personality assessments. While they can help gain self-awareness, they should not be used to label or limit ourselves. We are much more than any set of personality traits because our potential for growth and change is limitless.

So, with an awareness of the benefits and limitations of personality traits, let us explore the five dimensions of the Big 5 Personality assessment. You can go to https://bigfive-test.com[1] to do a free assessment to find out where you play around in the 5 dimensions. First, I explain what they are.

Big 5 dimensions

There are many personality assessment tools available. Famous ones are the Big 5, Myers-Briggs, the DISC assessment, and so on. I like the straightforwardness of the Big 5.

The Big Five personality dimensions are also known as the Five-Factor Model. The five dimensions are:

1. **Openness to experience**: This reflects a person's willingness to try new things and their level of creativity and curiosity. People with high openness tend to have a variety of interests as well as original ideas. Those who are low in openness tend to possess expert knowledge about a job, topic, or subject while possessing a down-to-earth, here-and-now view of the present.

1. **Conscientiousness**: This refers to a person's level of organisation, responsibility and self-discipline. Conscientiousness also refers to the degree to which we push towards goals at work. High Conscientiousness refers to a

---

1.   https://bigfive-test.com/

person who tends to work towards goals in an industrious, disciplined and dependable fashion. Low Conscientiousness refers to one who tends to approach goals in a relaxed, spontaneous and open-ended fashion. Such people are usually capable of multi-tasking and being involved in many projects and goals at the same time.

2. **Extraversion**: This reflects a person's level of sociability, assertiveness and energy level. Extraversion refers to the degree to which a person can tolerate sensory stimulation from people and situations. Those who score high on extraversion are characterized by their preference for being around other people and being involved in many activities. Low extraversion is characterised by one's preference to work alone and is typically described as a serious, sceptical, quiet and private person.

3. **Agreeableness**: This refers to a person's level of kindness, empathy and cooperation with others. It refers to the degree to which we relate to others. High agreeableness describes a person who tends to relate to others by being tolerant, agreeable and accepting. Low agreeableness describes someone who tends to relate to others by being expressive, tough, guarded, persistent, competitive or aggressive. Low-agreeable people may not accept information without checking it, and may come across to others as hostile, rude, self-centred, and not a team player.

4. **Neuroticism:** Better described as Emotional Stability, so as not to confuse it with pathological neuroticism which is described as a core personality trait characterized by emotional instability, irritability, anxiety, self-doubt, depression and other negative feelings. This dimension reflects a person's level of emotional stability and resilience, as well as their tendency towards anxiety and negative emotions.

Another way to understand this is that the *need for stability* refers to the degree to which a person responds to stress. More resilient people tend to handle stressful situations in a calm, steady and secure way. More reactive personas tend to respond in an alert, concerned, attentive or excitable way, thus creating the opportunity to experience more stress than others.

Each of these dimensions exists on a continuum, meaning that people can fall anywhere along the spectrum for each trait. It is also important to note that not one dimension is inherently better or worse than another. Each trait has its strengths and weaknesses, and different combinations of traits can be advantageous in different situations.

This reminds me of something Carl Jung said: "I would rather be whole than good."

The quote refers to Jung's belief that there are things in our psyche that are suppressed or rejected and that it is precisely these things that need to be acknowledged and integrated. This leads to a "whole" self, which is preferable to simply being good.

It reflects the yin-yang concept that sees life as filled with complementary forces. Forces that are not static or mutually exclusive. They coexist and can transform into each other under certain conditions. The yin-yang symbol is that of an ever-moving line that becomes a turning circle. Communicating a worldview of life as motion or movement as opposed to being stuck.

Back to Jung's idea that I would rather be whole than good. Wholeness over goodness highlights a crucial distinction between striving for goodness and embracing wholeness. Rather than merely conforming to societal norms or pursuing an idealized version of ourselves, Jung suggests that true growth and fulfilment come from integrating all aspects of our psyche. A bit like the sumptuous dish Mia makes for her family.

Being whole means acknowledging both our light and our shadow sides, our conscious and unconscious elements. It's an act of relinquishing control and accepting our full range of experiences. Jung cautioned against heroically sacrificing our inner impulses for an idealised self-image. A friend explained this beautifully. If you are naturally right-handed, doing things with your left hand will result in suboptimal performance.

There is also the danger that when we suppress our darker aspects in pursuit of goodness, we can be on our way to a mental breakdown. This is exactly the opposite of resilience. Wholeness requires acceptance, listening, and integration of both sides of our personality.

Conclusion

Okay. Like Liam, we have covered an ocean of water. Let's see if I can pull all the ropes to hoist the sails together.

We are still busy with the first building block for being resilient (positive self-esteem.) We broke positive self-esteem up into three elements. In the first chapter, we looked at taking control of the story we tell ourselves. In this chapter, we considered how to accept our strong and weak points. We explained how we all fit into a hierarchy and that, in this hierarchy, we naturally compare ourselves with others. Our main argument is that to be resilient, we need to constantly update this comparison software that is running in the background.

From the number of ways to update this software, we explore personality traits to showcase our uniqueness. Ending with the great advice of Carl Jung that we should strive to be whole rather than just good. We should, as Mia illustrated, make a delicious meal of all our aspects. In the upcoming chapters, we look at some of the other ways to update our comparison software.

We bring this unit to a close by retelling our stories in such a way that our self-esteem flourishes. We do this by making peace with our past.

Chapter 3 – Making Peace with Our Past

"To be human is to have a story to tell. A human being is nothing but a story with skin around it." (Fred Allen)

Introduction

This is the last of three chapters exploring self-acceptance. Self-acceptance is the first foundation stone that has to be in place to be able to live with resilience.

As you may have noticed, storytelling is the common theme in all the chapters. It relates to our belief systems, the stories we tell ourselves of how the world is supposed to work. We evaluated these belief systems to see if they serve us well. We considered comparisons and how to celebrate our diversity and the unique place we hold in society's hierarchy.

In this chapter, we wrap up the storytelling theme by taking the initiative to tell our story the way it works for us.

We first evaluate our history. Then we look at common themes, and lastly, identify possible pitfalls before we create a story that makes peace with who we are.

Let us explore how to be the author of our life.

Evaluating our history

We all have a history that we can tell as a story. These stories support our beliefs and give our life meaning. Stories give us a sense of belonging as they connect us with our ancestors and old heroes. We tell our stories in such a way that they keep us and our world stable and predictable.

A critical step in building resilience is to first become aware of the life story that has governed our lives. Our self-esteem is formed throughout our lives and is strongly influenced by events. To make peace with our past we need to go back to those events that formed our self-esteem and re-evaluate them.

I want to pause for a moment. For some people, this can be a difficult or traumatic experience, so I recommend that they seek professional help in the form of a psychologist or therapist when doing these exercises.

For most of us, this might just be uncomfortable and hopefully liberating. As we saw in Chapter One, we change ourselves by changing our beliefs about ourselves; we do this by constructively retelling our stories. Constructively retelling our stories will enable us to make peace. To get to this point we will have to look at the past with an open mind and explore the effects and/or consequences of our past experiences.

The aim of looking back into the past is firstly to identify the significant events that formed our self-esteem, and secondly to look for themes in our story that guide our perceptions.

There are many ways to tell our story. We can break it up in seven-year cycles, decades or maybe in developmental phases, like childhood, adolescence, etc. You can choose which way works best. In the eLearning course that goes with this book, we write down significant events and people that played a role, positive or negative, on a timeline broken up over decades.

Reflecting on identifying the formative events in our lives, we need to rely on memory. Memory is a tricky thing. Research has shown that memory is not a passive process but rather an active construction that relies on attention, motivation and association.[viii] Factors that affect memory recall are how long ago the memory was formed, if the information was elaborately reviewed and if any new information has disrupted or distorted the memory that the person is trying to recall. This means that every time you remember something it is influenced by the current context you are in. Your mood, immediate environment, other people's presence and current events. Your memory of an event is constantly updated.

The Indian writer Rabindranath Tagore reminds us in *My Reminiscences*:[ix]

> I know not who paints the pictures on memory's canvas; but whoever he may be, what he is painting are pictures; by which I mean that he is not there with his brush simply to make a faithful copy of all that is happening. He takes in and leaves out according to his taste. He makes many a big thing small and small thing big. He has no compunction in putting into the background that which was to the fore, or bringing to the front that which was behind. In short he is painting pictures, and not writing history.

I share this with you to invite you to release the weight of significance we place on memory. Our memory is very important. A big part of our identity is embedded in our memory. So, respect your memory (and that of others). Just know that it is relative and dynamic and like a garden, it should be taken care of.

Pitfalls to avoid

When reviewing our life stories, there are also common pitfalls. We will cover two of them and suggest ways to avoid them. The two pitfalls are attribution bias and cognitive dissonance.

When we reflect on the people in our history, it is easy to fall into an attribution bias.

Attribution bias is a cognitive bias that describes the tendency for people to make assumptions about the causes of other people's behaviour.

Specifically, attribution bias refers to the tendency to overemphasize internal, dispositional factors (such as personality or character) when explaining the behaviour of others, while underemphasizing external, situational factors (such as the context or environment).

For example, if someone cuts you off in traffic, you might assume that they are a rude or aggressive person (internal attribution) rather than considering the possibility that they might be in a hurry, distracted, or reacting to a dangerous situation on the road (external attribution).

There are two main types of attribution bias:

1. Fundamental Attribution Error (FAE): This bias occurs when we overemphasize personality (internal) factors and underestimate situational (external) factors when explaining the behaviour of others. FAE is particularly strong when we observe negative behaviours in others, such as aggression, rudeness or dishonesty.

1. Self-Serving Bias (SSB): This bias occurs when we take credit for our successes by attributing them to personality factors (such as talent, skill or effort) while attributing our failures to external factors (such as bad luck or difficult circumstances). SSB helps protect our self-esteem by maintaining a positive self-image, but it can also lead to overconfidence and complacency.

Being aware of this bias when we evaluate our history helps. It allows us to be honest about our role in remembering events. Being honest in this way enables you to take ownership of your story, because you realize you are the one attributing meaning to an event. If you are the author, you can re-write the story.

The second pitfall is cognitive dissonance, which we touched on earlier. There is a good chance for someone evaluating their history to experience cognitive dissonance - a psychological experience that occurs when we hold two or more beliefs, attitudes or values that are in conflict with each other. This creates a feeling of discomfort or tension, known as dissonance, which we feel compelled to resolve. Cognitive dissonance can be a powerful force that can motivate us to change our behaviour or beliefs, but it can also lead to confusion, self-doubt and internal conflict.

Put simply, in the story we tell ourselves we are normally the good person. When information comes our way that says otherwise, we become uncomfortable with the information (the dissonance) and either deal with it or ignore it. Some people also project it onto others. We cover projections in more detail in a later chapter. For now, all we need to know is that cognitive dissonance might happen and that we deal with it by keeping an open mind, slowing down our judgements, and waiting until the next time we look at the facts before we finalise our conclusions.

Waiting until the next time you see a person before you form a final opinion about them is a good habit to cultivate. Behind this habit is the understanding that people (ourselves included) only present a snippet of who they are at any given moment and that life is generally more complicated and has more shades of grey than what we can see in a singular event or moment. This habit creates space for cognitive dissonance to dissolve itself. Things are often not what they seem.

For example, when I met one of my dear friends for the first time, I saw him as stern and aloof. Getting to know him better over time, I learned that he is an introvert like me, and a lovely philosopher. We spend hours chatting about the complexities of life. Reflecting on this now, others might experience me in the same way the first time they meet me. This is food for thought.

Anyway... Why do we need to have this background information? Well, it will be useful when we evaluate our history and the people who played a role in forming our self-esteem.

For example, when we remember something that someone did that significantly influenced us, and we are aware of our contribution bias and cognitive dissonance, we can refer to an adage known as Hanlon's razor to mitigate the effect of these two biases.

Hanlon's razor is a saying or expression named after the author Robert J. Hanlon: "Never attribute to malice that which is adequately explained by incompetence." (The quote is sometimes attributed to Napoleon Bonaparte, but there is no definitive evidence that he said this.)

The concept behind the quote is that it is often more productive and accurate to assume that someone's actions were due to incompetence or ignorance rather than malicious intent. In other words, it's better to give people the benefit of the doubt and assume that they meant well but made a mistake, rather than assuming they had harmful intentions. In this way, Hanlon's razor helps us counter attribution bias and cognitive dissonance. It also helps to remember the rule we discussed in the first chapter: "Nothing anybody says or does is because of you."

The second goal of reviewing our past is to identify themes in our story. Themes can be seen as repeating patterns. Recognising the pattern makes it possible to change it. Let us explore possible themes that are common in people's stories.

Common story themes

Storytelling has evolved into a beautiful art form. Whether it is as a novel, a good movie or our favourite television series, some people have made successful careers in storytelling, and we can learn a lot from them.

For example, in literature, there are common themes in stories. There is the "Triumph Over Adversity" story, where the result is a success, no matter what obstacles you find in your way. Then there is the "Survival" theme. A survival story not only tells the tale of how someone escaped a challenging situation but also about the rest of their life and what events equipped them with the skills and mindset to pull through. Other themes are "Friends and Family", "Coming of Age", "Never Growing Up", "Accepting Change", and more. Do any of these themes resonate with your life story?

Narrative psychologists have also identified six universal life themes that emerged through their research. These themes are Love, Personal Value, Power, Freedom, Truth and Justice.

For each of these themes, the researchers identify whether the theme is present or absent in a person's life, and when present, whether the person accepts or integrates the theme. For example, someone may have lived in a loving supportive family environment, but because they see themselves as unlovable, they do not allow the love available to penetrate their being.

This can become complicated. Maybe there is an aspect in your story where one of these themes, like love or freedom, was absent. Once you have identified the theme, you can start exploring its consequences. These themes also give you a departure point to re-tell your story constructively.

Another common theme structure is that of archetypes. Archetypes are universal patterns that reflect our collective human experience. It transcends time, place, and even language. Appearing in many different forms, archetypes allow us to express and understand the storylines of our lives. Through them, we tell the tales of our tragedies and triumphs; our weaknesses and strengths; and the life chapters that are a part of our soul's evolution. So, when we are talking about shared patterns of thought, feeling, belief or behaviour, we are referring to archetypes. They are like giants in a story.

There are five universal archetypes: the Noble, the Victim, the Fighter, the Saviour and the Martyr.

The Noble one is the child inside of you who is forever young – never wanting to grow old. The noble one is playful, adventurous, and even mocking.

To the Victim, the world is an unfair place, where feelings, needs and wants are either ignored or unwelcome. More than simply knowing what it feels like to be mistreated and abused, the victim expects to be devalued. Victims are "poor me" people.

The Fighter archetype is present in people who are perpetually going against the grain. Fighters believe in a cause (or two) and want to have their point of view heard. Fighters hold their beliefs to be the truth ("the way it is") and often will fervently explain their position to ensure that you understand and ultimately agree with them.

The Saviour archetype takes hold of people who are naturally inclined to be caretakers. The saviour is overflowing with a desire to be helpful and always reliable in a crisis. Saviours frequently express their sympathy for those in distress and often become over involved in the lives of others. Saviours define themselves through their charitable pursuits and believe their hearts to be guided only by noble intentions.

The Martyr archetype is expressed by those who are filled with passion and a sense of purpose. Like the fighter archetype, martyrs align with a cause and work tirelessly toward furthering their mission, often at the cost of their well-being. Martyrs are often unconventional in their belief system, firmly standing in opposition to a more established perspective or mode of operation. There is a rebellious spirit in the martyr's blood that compels them to question authority and fearlessly oppose any injustice.

Do you recognise any of these characters in your own story?

Retelling your story

I suggest we use two lenses when retelling our history: gratitude and forgiveness.

I find people have misconceptions about both lenses. So, let's unpack them. Gratitude, like all great truths, is simple in its presentation and, at the same time, has a complex depth that is seldom exhausted. It starts with a simple "thank you" for what you have received in life, and then it snowballs from there if you allow it.

Gratitude is a powerful and positive emotion that involves recognizing and appreciating the good things in our lives. It is an attitude of thankfulness and a recognition of the value and kindness received from others or the world around us. "If the only prayer you ever say in your entire life is thank you, it will be enough," said the mystic and philosopher Meister Eckhart (c1260–1327).

Gratitude involves being aware of and acknowledging the positive aspects of our lives, both big and small. It is about recognizing the things we often take for granted, such as good health, supportive relationships, access to resources, a sunset, a flower or moments of joy.

By cultivating awareness of our blessings, we can shift our focus from what is lacking to what is present. Instead of dwelling on what is wrong or missing, it encourages us to focus on what is right and present. For example, when facing a challenging situation, gratitude helps us find silver linings or lessons to be learned, allowing us to approach difficulties with a more positive and resilient mindset.

Research has shown that practising gratitude can have a significant impact on our well-being. Regularly expressing gratitude has been linked to increased happiness, improved mental health, reduced stress levels and stronger relationships. By consciously cultivating gratitude, we can enhance our overall sense of contentment and life satisfaction.

It allows us to savour the present moment, cherish the relationships we have, and find joy in the simple pleasures of life.

I share these thoughts with you to encourage you to be grateful for the positive events and people that make up part of your history. I invite you not to underestimate the consequences of these positive inputs. You are who you are because of the dividends paid out of these positive investments. We all have a lot to be grateful for.

Next, let's explore forgiveness. Forgiveness is the antidote to all the negative events in our history.

Forgiveness is a complex and powerful concept that involves letting go of negative emotions, resentment, and the desire for revenge toward someone who has wronged us. It is an intentional and conscious choice to release ourselves from the emotional burden of anger and resentment.

Here are some key points to help you understand forgiveness:

1. Acknowledging the hurt: Forgiveness does not mean denying

or minimising the pain caused by someone's actions. It is important to acknowledge and validate your feelings of hurt, anger or betrayal. Recognising the impact of wrongdoing allows you to process your emotions and move towards healing.

1. Choosing to let go: Forgiveness is a voluntary act. It is a decision to let go of negative emotions and release the person who wronged you. It does not necessarily mean condoning or forgetting the actions, but rather freeing yourself from the emotional weight that can consume you.

2. Empathy and understanding: Developing empathy and trying to understand the perspective of the person who hurt you can be an important part of forgiveness. This doesn't justify their actions but helps you gain a broader understanding of the circumstances, motivations, or struggles they might have faced. Empathy can humanize the person and contribute to the process of forgiveness.

3. Healing and personal growth: Forgiveness is a powerful tool. By forgiving, you create space for emotional healing, letting go of the negative energy that can hinder your well-being and happiness. It allows you to focus on your own growth, rather than being consumed by resentment or seeking revenge.

4. Setting boundaries: Forgiving someone does not mean that you have to maintain or reestablish a relationship with them. It's essential to set healthy boundaries and prioritize your well-being. Depending on the situation, forgiveness may or may not lead to reconciliation or trust being restored.

5. Self-forgiveness: In addition to forgiving others, it is crucial to extend forgiveness to yourself. We all make mistakes and carry regrets. Self-forgiveness involves acknowledging our own imperfections, learning from our mistakes and treating

ourselves with compassion and understanding.

6. Time and process: Forgiveness is not always an immediate or linear process. It can take time, reflection and self-care to work through the emotions and reach a place of forgiveness. It's a journey unique to each individual and situation. Sometimes we have to repeat the act of forgiving over and over like watering a plant till it breaks through the soil.

Remember that forgiveness is a personal choice, and it may not always be easy. It is a gift you give to yourself, allowing you to find peace and move forward.

Conclusion

I conclude this chapter with a story of a man and a whale I heard years ago at a seminar on relationships.

So, this guy goes on his summer vacation. He has been working hard the whole year and saved up for his ideal vacation at the sea. For months he has been looking forward to the sun and the sea, and taking his boat out to do some fishing. On the first day of his vacation, he takes the boat out. And it is a perfect day. The sun is warm, there is a slight breeze to cool him down and the sea is calm. Best of all the fish are happy to be caught. He sits back and soaks in everything. It is better than he dreamed of.

As he sits blissfully happy, something bumps against his boat. And then again. He jumps up. Furious that his perfect day is being spoiled. But there is no other boat around, so he looks over the side of his boat and sees a whale.

He is so angry with the whale for spoiling his day, he grabs a harpoon gun used for spearfishing and shoots the whale in the back.

The whale doesn't notice and keeps on swimming. The man keeps a good grip on the harpoon and gets pulled after the whale as it swims deeper into the ocean. At some point, the whale decides to dive deep.

The man now has a choice. Does he hang on to the harpoon and go down with the whale or does he let go of the harpoon?

To forgive is to let go of the harpoon.

What would you do?

"If you are too weak to give yourselves your own law, then a tyrant shall lay his yoke upon you and say: 'Obey! Clench your teeth and obey!' And all good and evil shall be drowned in obedience to him" (Friedrich Nietzsche)

Chapter 4 – Owning Your Authority

Introduction

In this chapter of Part 2, we introduce the concept of autonomy. First, we explore why this is important. Then we make sure we have a clear understanding of what autonomy is. Lastly, we discuss a tool that can help us develop this strength.

Years ago, my wife and I were vacationing in the picturesque Hogsback village nestled in the Amathole Mountains in South Africa. As we meandered through the tourist shops, I came face to face with a shocking realization that I did not believe in my own authority. I was standing in a craft shop contemplating whether or not I should buy a trinket to remind me of the time we'd had in Hogsback. I wanted to be able to relive the good times, yet knew from experience that trinkets end up in a box or drawer, just to be thrown away in the future. Arguing with myself about wasting money or remembering good times, it suddenly dawned on me why I was so reluctant to take initiative. Deep down, I have this script running that I had no belief in my own authority. In essence, I realised that day I had no sense of agency and had not established my autonomy.

The belief in our authority – the power to execute – seems to be interwoven into our sense of agency and autonomy. And to be resilient is to have agency and autonomy.

I have an image in my head of me being the director who determines which actor does or says what on stage. Some people do not fully take up the directorship. They allow other people or circumstances to dictate what the actors (their thoughts and/or emotions) do. To become competent directors, we need to explore and understand personal authority as sourced from our agency and autonomy.

Since that day in Hogsback, I have been working on this insight and the result of this work is what I share with you in this chapter.

Why is autonomy important?

For us to be able to deal with life's challenges, living with autonomy is a key competency to build up resilience. Someone highly competent in living with autonomy is a person who is self-determining and independent. That person can resist social pressures, regulate their behaviour from within, and evaluate their sense of self by their own personal standards.

In contrast, someone with low autonomy competency is a person who is concerned about the expectations and evaluations of others. They rely on the judgements of others to make important decisions and conform to social pressures to think and act in certain ways.

In today's fast-paced world where everyone's role isn't as clearly defined, it is crucial to navigate diverse demands effectively. To thrive in various aspects – be it at work, with family, or socially – it's essential to take up the oars like Liam and make independent choices. And when we do, magic happens. The fish arrive.

Figure 3- https://www.linkedin.com/pulse/sailing-story-you-cant-change-wind-adjust-sails-ana-serra/

"And then, without warning, God decides to treat us with the Perfect Wind! In compliance, we hear our Captain shouting "Spiegare le vele!" (Hoist the sails).

He starts freeing the ropes that up until then had been strangling its sails, denying her freedom. I have no words for that exact instant.

*That same boat that had been forced to hold its breath all this time is finally gasping for air. And we are here to experience this magical moment. The sailing boat in all its glory. The sails that once were unjustly incarcerated are now majestically standing and leading the way, maneuvered solely by God's given wind, ropes, and a man who knows exactly what to do. We are now one with what surrounds us. It is at that precise moment that you hear nature speaking to you... and you listen. This magical energy is just sublime. It triggers our emotions to another level. We are **Sailing.***

The ability to choose and act freely is fundamental to our sense of well-being. If someone or a situation takes away our freedom to choose, we wither. We strongly dislike such circumstances. If you look at the tragedies throughout history, it normally has to do with people's autonomy being taken away from them. Examples are slavery and prisoner-of-war camps.

Contrast this with when we are given a choice. We are more open to people or situations. We engage more and take more ownership of what is happening. In our lives and in our dealing with other people, we need to understand this concept well.

Clarifying the concept

To integrate this competency, we need to distinguish between agency and autonomy.

Agency is the ability to act independently and make one's own choices. It is the capacity to be an agent or a person who can act.

Autonomy is the state of being self-governing. It is the ability to make decisions and act on those decisions without being controlled by others.

We can put it this way. Agency is the ability to act, while autonomy is the ability to act freely. Agency is a necessary condition for autonomy, but it is not sufficient. In other words, you can have agency without having autonomy, but you cannot have autonomy without having agency.

Agency is a social construct.[x] It is not something that we are born with, but rather something that we learn through our interactions with others. It is dictated by our cultural environment. Someone in a liberal culture will have a different understanding of their agency than someone in a traditional culture. It is wise to keep this in mind when relating to other people.

Frank Delano, the director of a programme for girls at a residential centre in the US, tells the story of 16-year-old Aleksandra from Russia whose parents were institutionalised due to mental illness.[xi] Her uncle, Vladimir, single and overwhelmed, hired a housekeeper for her younger brother and placed Aleksandra in the group home, adamant about her becoming a doctor. Aleksandra, also overwhelmed with the loss of her parents and living in a new culture, was struggling academically. Her uncle's expectations were unrealistic.

Despite the staff's attempts, Vladimir refused to engage. A candid conversation during a special lunch with Aleksandra revealed her uncle's cultural beliefs and his reluctance to meet with female staff.

She explained that Vladimir saw culture in the United States as empty and unsophisticated. Frank continued to probe and asked what her uncle wanted to do with them on weekends to relax. Aleksandra said he insisted they should be going to "the ballet so they could be more culturally sophisticated."

Learning from Aleksandra about their struggles and Vladimir's sentiments, Frank invited Vladimir to a ballet performance. The event marked a turning point, leading to productive meetings with Vladimir, and a more realistic approach to Aleksandra's future.

This story exemplifies the importance of cultural understanding in addressing family dynamics and ensuring the well-being of children in care.

The way we are raised influences our sense of agency.

Agency is limited. There are some things that we cannot control, and we need to be aware of these limits to make good decisions. It helps to think of your circle of influence. Inside the circle are the things you can control, which boils down to the choices you make and the actions you initiate. Everything else is outside your circle of influence – the weather, other people's emotions, their choices, etc. The AA serenity prayer fits perfectly here: "God, grant me the serenity to accept the things I cannot change, the courage to change the things I can, and the wisdom to know the difference."

Autonomy is important for living a good life. It allows us to live according to our own values and beliefs. We look at our value system in an upcoming chapter. Autonomy requires individuals to be allowed to manage their lives in meaningful and responsible ways by exercising control over their living and working conditions.

In general, autonomy requires an orientation toward the future and an awareness of one's environment, social dynamics, and the roles one plays and wants to play. It assumes the possession of a sound self-concept and the ability to translate needs and wants into acts of will: decision, choice and action.

Now that we have a clearer understanding of what autonomy is, let's take the next step and ask. How do we develop this competency?

49

Autonomy quadrants

A friend of mine, who has been a pilot his whole life, explained to me how pilots and control towers use radar.

Radar is a system that uses radio waves to detect objects. In aviation, radar is used to track aeroplanes and keep them safe from each other. Radar works by sending out a beam of radio waves. When the waves hit an object, they bounce back to the radar antenna. The radar then measures the time it takes for the waves to travel to the object and back and uses this information to calculate the object's distance, speed and direction.

Radar is essential for air traffic control. It helps controllers to keep track of all the planes in the airspace and to ensure that they are flying safely and efficiently.

An analogy that might help you understand how radar works is to imagine you're in a dark room. You want to know if there's anything in the room. You could throw a ball into the room and listen for it to bounce back. If you hear a bounce, you know there's something in the room. Radar works similarly, except instead of throwing a ball, it sends out radio waves.

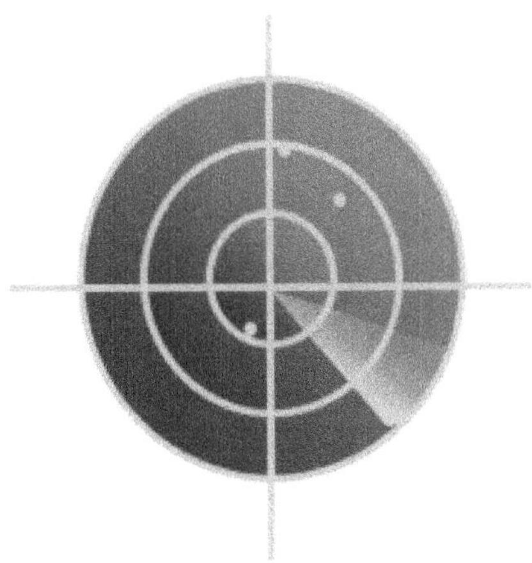

• • • •

Pilots and air traffic controllers read the radio waves on a screen with concentric circles and dots. The circles are the distance the wave travels and the dots are the airplanes.

I use this radar analogy to introduce a thinking tool I developed to assist in growing our autonomy competency.

Two concepts are important in this tool and together they build our autonomy. Our locus of control and locus of causality.

Locus of control (*locus* is Latin for a place or location) refers to our fundamental belief about where the authority or power to act out our lives resides. It asks who has control. It can be any place on a continuum between external and internal locus. If we have an external locus of control, we believe that some external force (person or situation) has control. We believe we have control when we have an internal locus of control.

Whereas locus of control asks where things are controlled from, locus of causality asks from where things develop. It is also on an internal-external continuum.

An internal locus of causality belief system says, "I make things happen" and an external locus of causality belief system says, "Things happen to me."

Remember that this is a dynamic continuum and on this continuum is an important circle of influence. For example, you and I have no control over the weather. Whether it rains or not is totally outside our control, but we do choose what to wear when it rains. Our choice of gear falls inside our circle of influence. People with an external locus of control tend to complain that the rain prevents them from having a fun day. People with an internal locus of control have fun dancing in the rain.

To illustrate the power of this concept I invite you to read Victor Frankl's *Man's Search for Meaning*.[xii] He was a psychiatrist who survived the Nazi concentration camps. In his book, he explains how they could predict who'd survive the day and who would not, based on their sense of agency. He also shares a personal story of how he could endure the whipping of the guards because he kept his locus of control internal. If it was possible for him to apply this mindset in those hellish circumstances, how much more possible is it not for us to do so in our day-to-day challenges?

In thinking about these concepts, I created a thinking tool I call the Autonomy Quadrants.[xiii]I combined the two concepts, locus of control and causality by placing them on two continuums as an x- and y-axis. This then forms four quadrants. Please note that in explaining the different quadrants I overgeneralise to emphasise a point. Real life involves a range of nuances.

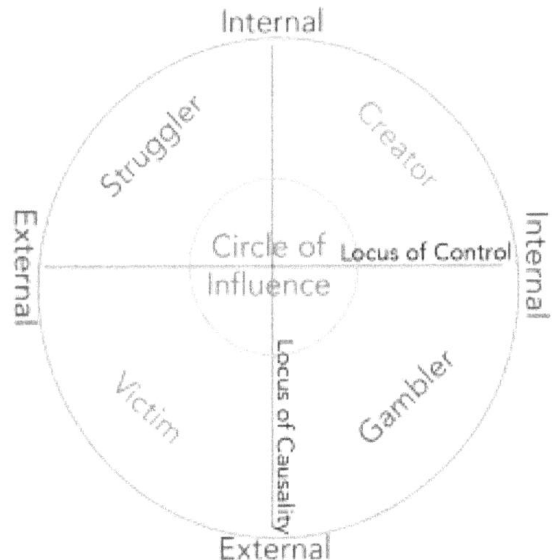

The locus of control continuum is placed on the x-axis with the internal pole on the right and the external pole on the left. The locus of causality becomes the y-axis with the internal pole at the top and the external pole at the bottom. Let's explore each one of these quadrants.

The victim quadrant. External locus of control and causality. People who fall into this quadrant believe that some external power or person has control over what happens to them. They are powerless as things keep on happening to them. They have a strong victim mentality and tend to be stuck in the drama of this quadrant. It seems bad luck always follows them around. I notice that at some point they get addicted to the drama. So much so that they create the drama to experience the pity associated with it. Don't go there.

The struggler quadrant. External locus of control and internal locus of causality. People in this quadrant have a sense of their ability to make things happen, but they are always locked in a struggle against the powers that be. Because their locus of control is external (an external entity holds the authority), they tend to be easily influenced by the current situation. But they are always ready to act according to what they believe is important. People in this quadrant easily blame a named or unnamed external power (a secret society or autocratic authority) for some evil and then organise (initiate action) a rally against it.

In the third quadrant, we find **the gambler**. Internal locus of control and external locus of causality. People who have a sense of control over their reactions, but because their causality is external, they live with a mentality that whatever hand of cards life deals them, they will make the best of it. They easily go with the flow of things and deal with whatever comes their way. This is a reactive way of living, and they need to learn how to take the initiative and make things happen for themselves.

I call people in the last quadrant, **creators.** Internal locus of control and causality. They have a sense of their authority to control their reactions and a belief in their ability to make things happen. They are the creators of their lives. I believe this is the healthiest quadrant and that we all need to grow this mentality.

To understand this mode, it is important to know and accept that there is a definite circle of influence in the centre of these four quadrants.

There are events that we have no control over. For example, in 2011 an earthquake and tsunami hit Japan. There was no way the Japanese could control or cause this disaster. They were legitimate victims. But they quickly moved to the creator quadrant to rebuild what was destroyed. So should we when an accident happens. This model is dynamic, and we do not have to be stuck in one quadrant. Move! Activate your locus of control and causality from within (internal) as quickly as you can and create the reality that you want.

Conclusion

Let's wrap up. To be competent in being autonomous, see yourself as the pilot of your life. Use the radar of the four autonomy quadrants to fly in the creator quadrant as much as possible. If by chance the weather drives you to one of the other quadrants, re-adjust and get back on track. Follow the example of Liam in the opening story, or the words of William Henley in Invictus:

Invictus

Out of the night that covers me,
Black as the pit from pole to pole,
I thank whatever gods may be
For my unconquerable soul.
In the fell clutch of circumstance
I have not winced nor cried aloud.
Under the bludgeonings of chance
My head is bloody, but unbowed.
Beyond this place of wrath and tears
Looms but the Horror of the shade,
And yet the menace of the years
Finds, and shall find, me unafraid.
It matters not how strait the gate,
How charged with punishments the scroll,
I am the master of my fate:
I am the captain of my soul.

Chapter 5 – When Actions Speak the Loudest

Introduction

In the chapter on autonomy, we discussed the impact of self-authority (made up of our agency) as the ability to choose, and our autonomy as the ability to choose freely.

In this chapter, we follow up on this truth with a question. What influences our choices?

We can share a long conversation about how nature and nurture play a role and how the media and our needs influence us. However, I hope to clarify things by exploring how our values influence our choices. Or how they should influence our choices to become more resilient.

My dad used to quote Ralph Waldo Emerson's words, "What you do speaks so loudly I cannot hear what you are saying." What we do, the action we take is the result of what we choose to be the most important at any given time. We all know those people who say, "Let's grab a cup of coffee soon" but it never happens. If we ask them about it, they will probably say, "Sorry, I have been very busy."

The truth is, it was not that important to them to spend time with us. Whatever they chose to do in the time they had, was more important than coffee with us. The point is our actions show our true colours.

It is always our actions that move the needle. We can talk about what we are going to do, exercising for example. But unless we physically move our bodies nothing will change.

It is better to pay attention to what people actually do than to what they say. This is also true for us. What we actually do, reflects what is important. What is important to us is motivated by what we value – our value system.

Clarifying the concept

A man was conned by a woman's story about a sick child. He gave her money. When he found out he had been conned and that there was no sick child, he exclaimed, "I'm so glad."

What does his response say about his values? What would your response be?

What are Values? Values are individual beliefs that motivate people to act one way or another. They serve as a guide for human behaviour. Like morals, they help you to distinguish right from wrong.

Values in a narrow sense are that which is good, desirable or worthwhile. They are the motive behind purposeful action. Values are fundamental beliefs that guide or qualify your conduct, interaction with others, search for meaning and involvement in your career.

Generally, people are predisposed to adopt the values that they are raised with. People also tend to believe that those values are "right" because they are the values of their particular culture. In this way, values are society's shared beliefs about what is good or bad and how people should act.

And because all of us live in a society, we all have values. Most of us are not even aware of what we value because we have never thought about this. But they are there in the background, driving our behaviour And to grow in our resilience to deal with life's challenges, it is better to know what drives our behaviour than to be on autopilot.

Multidimensional characteristics and principles

There are as many value systems as there are people. We can classify them into five categories:

1. Personal values define you as an individual. Honesty,

reliability and trust determine how you will face the world and relate to people.

1. Spiritual values are formed by your religion or belief in God or a Higher Being. These values influence your ethics and perception of the value of life in general.
2. Cultural values, like the practice of your faith and customs, sustain connections with your cultural roots. They help you feel connected to a larger community of people with similar backgrounds.
3. Social values indicate how you relate meaningfully to others in social situations, including those involving family, friends and co-workers.
4. Work values guide your behaviour in professional contexts. They define how you work and how you relate to your co-workers, bosses and clients. They also reveal your potential for advancement.

To make things even more interesting, values do not come in one size fits all. Conflicting values can co-exist in one person's value system. Let me explain.

In the game of golf there are broadly speaking three types of golf players. We get the put-put or mini golf players. They engage on the easiest level and will play on vacations with friends. The second type is the casual player. They actually set foot on the golf course. Play maybe once a month or every second week. Then, thirdly, there are the professionals. The game is their life. Their income. They are at it every day.

Each of these players lives in a house with different rooms. A living room, bedroom and bathroom. Each of these rooms holds different access rights. Most visitors have access to the living room. Only family or good friends have access to the bedroom, and we all go to the bathroom on our own.

Now, let's create a matrix with the players and their rooms. In the first column, you have the putt-putt player, the casual player and the pro. In the first row, you have the different rooms, bathroom, bedroom and living room.

Player/Room	Bathroom	Bedroom	Living room
Putt-Putt Player	Simple value	Simple value	Simple value
Casual Player	Complex Value	Simple/Complex Value	Simple value
Professional Player	Complex Value	Complex Value	Complex Value

We can now plot the use of values in this matrix. Let's take euthanasia, for example. The word "euthanasia" comes from the Greek words "eu" (good) and "thanatos" (death) so it's about the choice to end human life in the case of terminal illness and suffering. In most countries this is illegal. The put-put player will probably have the same values across all three rooms. These players normally accept the broader social values as the norm in every situation. They tend not to reflect on circumstances or any variable that might influence their opinion of their value system. For them, euthanasia is probably wrong.

The casual player might have a set of values for the more accessible rooms, and a different set for the private rooms. This is normally influenced by personal experiences and the understanding that not all things are created equal. For them, considering euthanasia for a mother or brother dying of cancer might be a consideration.

The pro player will probably have different value sets in every room. The medical doctor, for example, may strongly believe in preserving life, in the bathroom; at the same time, they see their patients suffering in the bedroom, and they need to adhere to the hospital or country policies in the living room.

Using this matrix as a guide for our value systems, we can keep our values flexible and resilient.

Why are values important?

Investing time and effort to uncover and articulate our personal values brings many important benefits:

Values can help reduce stress. Research studies have shown that those who think about their highest values before a stressful event actually experience less stress and show a substantial decrease in the stress hormone, cortisol, compared to control groups. Keeping your values in mind reminds you of what's important and puts the stressor into perspective.

Connecting with your values boosts decision-making and problem-solving skills. Meg Selig, the author of *Silver Sparks: Thoughts on growing older, wiser, and happier* shares:"When I've been faced with a difficult decision, I find that searching for the values underlying a particular choice can help me choose a path forward. I may not like the result of my decision, but at least I know "*why*" I made the choice, and focusing on my valued reasons counteracts regret and self-blame."[xiv]

It's easier to make choices between conflicting opportunities that arise – where to invest our time, what behaviour is most appropriate and where we need to concentrate our personal improvement efforts – when we are aware of our values.

Values charge up our willpower so we can persist in difficult tasks. Willpower means using the thought of our most important values and goals to guide our behaviour.

Values help us act more assertively. It is easier to be assertive when we are aware of what we stand for, and we are more likely to rise to our own defence when another person has violated our boundaries.

Values help you communicate with more compassion. Reflecting on your deepest values can also "create an inner state of intense awareness and calm," according to Newburg and Waldman, authors of *Words Can Change Your Brain*. This inner state can help us listen more intently to others and choose our words with tender loving care.

Knowing and acting on values bolsters our confidence and our self-identity. Our sense of security will be strengthened. It will provide the stable and solid core we need to transform the rapid changes coming at us, from terrifying threats to exciting opportunities.

Other benefits include making wiser career and work choices. Knowing and sharing our values enhances relationship intimacy.

The "how to"

So, how do we know what our guiding values are? In this next exercise I will guide you through a practical process of identifying your top values.

I invite you to imagine you and I are standing outside on the road. Between us is a train track. You are standing at the one end and I on the other. According to Google, one train track is 60 metres long, 10 centimetres high, and six centimetres wide.

In this exercise I want you to walk the 60 metres towards me balancing on top of the track. To motivate you to do so, I am willing to give you anything from $50-$100. Would you do it?

Most people would. It is easy money.

Now, let's make it more challenging. We go to a skyscraper. Thirty storeys high. We balance one end of the train track on the building, while the other end dangles from a helicopter hovering in the air. Now, do the same as before. Balance yourself (without safety equipment) and walk to the helicopter.

And because you will not do it for $100, I offer you $1 million. Would you, do it? Most people will not.

Now, imagine I take the person you love the most, a child or a partner or family member, with me in the helicopter. And I challenge you. If you do not walk over the train track, I will drop your beloved to the ground. Would you do it now?

Most of us would start crawling over the track, wouldn't we?

The point of the exercise is that there are some things so important to us, that we are willing to face death for them. These are our core values.

So, let's say we identified our core values. What now?

How do we take our values and make them concrete? How do we move them from ideals to which we strive to actionable day-to-day behaviour?

Remember my dad's favourite quote, "I can't hear what you are saying, because your actions speak too loudly." What you value, believe and think is transparent through your actions. The only way is to transform the vagueness into observable behaviour.

Here are steps to define measurable values: First, define clear, succinct values. Use the train track exercise to do this. Then give these values definitions. Describe what you mean when you say one of my values is, let's say, honesty. Make it clear so that when someone else reads it, they will understand immediately what you mean.

The next important step is adding behavioural examples that demonstrate each value. Identify at least three but no more than four, valued behaviours.

For example, let's say it is important to you that everybody is respectful towards each other. But what does respect mean? Respect in one culture is not the same as in another. For instance, making eye contact in one culture shows respect while in another it shows disrespect. So, you must clearly define what respect is in your life.

Let's say you define respect as "treating people with appreciation and dignity". Next, describe specific behaviours that display respect:

- I assume people have my best interest in mind, so I attack problems and processes, not people.

- I will say please and thank you when I request something from a colleague. I understand that they are busy with their responsibilities. They assist me because they choose to not because they must.

- When I disagree with someone, I will speak to them directly in private first and not gossip behind their back.

When you are considering behaviour, ask yourself: Is this an observable behaviour? Can people I work with observe, and/or listen to my interactions with others, and assess my demonstration of this behaviour?

Hopefully, you now have an idea of what your values are. Imagine acting on them. Try catching yourself doing them. Acknowledge yourself for living them. When you act outside your values, stop, forgive yourself and re-align again to be in the creator quadrant.

Conclusion

In a field, there was an oak at one end and a willow tree at the other. Whenever a wind moved through the field, the willow swayed in the wind, while the oak remained unmoved. When this happened, the willow said to itself, "I wish I was as strong as the oak, instead of bending over with every breeze." Then one day a large windstorm whipped through the field.

When the storm had passed, and the darkness lifted, the willow looked across the field and was shocked to discover that the oak was lying on the ground, broken. When the gardener came into the field, the willow said, "Oh, sir, what happened to the oak? How is it that I survived the storm, weak as I am, and the oak fell?"

The gardener said, "Oh little willow tree, do you not understand? When the winds blow, you bend with them, while the oak remains still. So, when a powerful wind comes along, you survive it. But the oak cannot bend and so if the wind is strong enough, it will break, for the oak had a secret, a weakness within that no one looking from the outside can see."

And the gardener went on his way, leaving the willow to ponder what he said.[xv]

Strength within and strength without are not the same, so we should cultivate strength within first. Also, when the winds blow, bend, and you may survive the real storms when they come. Try and resist them, and when the real storms come, you may break instead. And this is true for our value system. It should not be rigid but ever-evolving from the inside out.

Part 3 – Positive Relationships

"To be fully seen by somebody, then, and be loved anyhow - this is a human offering that can border on miraculous." (Elizabeth Gilbert)

Chapter 6 – Being Connected

Introduction

Take another look at our pyramid in the introduction. Chapter 6 is the start of the second tier. We have put in place powerful foundation stones of positive self-esteem and autonomy. In this chapter, we'll dive into the fascinating world of building strong connections with others. We aim to find out why and how we can create positive interpersonal relationships.

When it comes to relationships, there are different types and stages that we go through. It's like navigating through a labyrinth. A labyrinth is an intricate structure with winding pathways, often found in places of worship or holy sites. Unlike a maze, a labyrinth has no dead ends or puzzles to solve. It is a single path that leads you to the center and back out again.

The labyrinth is a powerful metaphor for relationships. Just as in a labyrinth, our relationships have twists and turns. Sometimes we feel like we're making progress, only to find ourselves back at the beginning. But that doesn't mean we are lost or going in circles. It's all part of the journey.

. . . .

Ultimately, every relationship leads to our relationship with ourselves. As Japanese novelist Haruki Murakami said, "Things outside you are a projection of what's inside you, and what's inside you is a projection of what's outside." So, when we step into the labyrinth of a relationship, we're also stepping into the labyrinth within ourselves.

Before we delve into this deeper connection, let's first explore the building blocks of interpersonal relationships. Understanding the different types of relationships and the stages they go through, is essential in cultivating positive connections with others. It's like laying a strong foundation for a remarkable building.

So, let's embark on this journey as we uncover the nuts and bolts of building positive interpersonal relationships. Remember, it's all about embracing the twists and turns, both within ourselves and with those around us. We'll navigate this labyrinth together and discover the joy of meaningful connections. Are you ready? Let's do this!

Why are positive relationships important?

One of the deepest psychological needs we humans have is the need to belong. It is an ingrained survival instinct, rooted in our earliest experiences of being connected to the world around us, like when we were in our mother's womb. We were safe, taken care of, and completely immersed in our environment.

But as soon as we were born that connection was shattered, and ever since then, we've been on a journey to reconnect and experience that sense of belonging again. It's so deeply established in our psyche that when we feel rejected, our brains register it as physical pain, like being stabbed with a knife. Incredible, right? Our brains can't distinguish between the pain of a physical wound and the pain of being rejected.

The importance of belonging dates back to prehistoric times, when being part of a tribe was crucial for our survival. We were better off collaborating and working together than trying to survive on our own. So, being banished from the tribe was one of the worst punishments. Kind of like being "cancelled" by social media, today!

Fast forward to the present, and it seems like we've lost that deep connection or lost touch with this experience. The importance of feeling connected and belonging is well-documented. Just look at the studies done on the "Blue Zones". These are communities where people not only live longer but enjoy a high quality of life in their old age. Their strong sense of community and connectedness with each other plays a major role in their well-being and longevity.

Harvard researchers conducted a study that started in the 1960s and is still ongoing. It confirms what we already know deep down: interpersonal relationships are crucial for our happiness and well-being. Good relationships with friends and family are the number one reason people report being happy.

We humans are happiest when we feel seen and acknowledged by others. When we know that we belong and that our value is recognised. Our sense of status and well-being is often directly related to our ability to feel included and connected with others.

Now, it's not rocket science to understand that good relationships are important in our professional or personal lives. But here's the reality: few people actually experience that meaningful connection. Why? Well, from the moment we are born, we navigate our sense of self in relation to others. As children, we rely on our caregivers, so we naturally adapt our behaviour to please them and ensure their acceptance and kindness.

As we grow older, we venture outside our primary caregivers and make friends. During adolescence especially, we start shaping our identity based on how our peers perceive us. This journey of self-formation and connection continues until late adulthood, when we often find ourselves wanting to give back and serve the larger community.

In this journey from birth to individuation and then back towards serving the community again, to fit in we reject some part of us. These rejected parts become our shadow. It is this self-rejection process that disconnects us from the whole and stands in the way of experiencing positive relationships with others. Self-acceptance is the road we take to experience connection with others. And that's why I love to use the labyrinth as a symbol for interpersonal relationships. It perfectly represents this movement and the intertwining of our lives with others.

Now that we understand the importance of connecting with people, let's talk about what positive interpersonal relationships could look like.

Imagine healthy and fulfilling connections built on trust, mutual respect and shared values. Relationships that involve effective communication, active listening and constructive approaches to resolving conflicts. Relationships that have clear boundaries, emotional intimacy and are nurtured over time and where the effort to build them is returned.

Positive interpersonal relationships are characterized by warmth, friendliness, genuine interest, empathy, and a desire to facilitate and support one another. They foster deeper connections, enhance understanding and contribute to our overall well-being and happiness.

Is this not what we all want?

Clarifying the concept – types and phases

To grow these positive relationships, it helps to know that there are different types. Each has its own fascinating connections to explore.

Understanding the differences helps us to create the necessary boundaries to manage our relationships effectively. Not all relationships are equal. Each one is unique and holds its own significance. As a friend of mine explained to his son. A healthy diet consists of the right proportions of greens, proteins and carbohydrates. In the same way, each type of relationship brings with it, in proportion, the nutrients for our well-being. And in this diversity of relationships, we find the threads that weave our lives together.

I find it helps to think of concentric circles radiating around and away from us. Closest to us are our family. These are the ties that bind us through blood, marriage, or adoption. They can be a source of immense love and support, but they can also be challenging and complex.

And then, the romantic relationships. These are the ones that make our hearts flutter and our knees weak. They are the connections we share with our partners, filled with passion and intimacy.

In the same ring are our friends. These are the people who share our interests, values and experiences. Friends come in all shapes and sizes, from casual acquaintances to those who become like family. They are there to laugh, cry and create memories with us.

Next, is the professional realm. Here, we encounter colleagues and business relationships. Colleagues can start as mere acquaintances but can turn into supportive friends who celebrate our successes and lend a helping hand during tough times. Business relationships are formed through mutual trust and respect, whether in transactions or partnerships.

Beyond the workplace, we enter the realm of shared interests and hobbies. We form these connections with individuals who have a common passion. Whether it's a club or a public organisation, these relationships can be casual and social or evolve into a tight-knit community with a shared purpose.

And lastly, we have the societal and neighbourhood relationships. These ties are formed with the people who live in our geographical area.

They can be as simple as friendly chats over the fence or as profound as working together for the betterment of the community we call home.

Thinking about the different types of relationships in concentric circles helps us to invest our energy and trust appropriately. We trust (or are supposed to trust) those closest to us more than those in the outer circle.

It also helps to know that every relationship goes through phases.

The several key phases that characterize interpersonal relationships typically include initiation, characterized by the initial contact and impression formation; growth, marked by increased intimacy and mutual understanding; maintenance, where relationships are sustained and developed; and finally, deterioration or dissolution, involving a decline in closeness or the termination.

Awareness of these phases contributes to more successful management of relationships. For example, we now know there is a termination phase in all relationships. This can be when a life partner of 60 years passes away or a fleeting sales transaction that ends in a few minutes. Knowing this, we can proactively invest energy and time to make sure our estate is in order before it is needed. At the same time not bother about the sales representative's comments.

Transitioning between phases can be accompanied by various emotional experiences, from the excitement of forming new connections to the challenges of adapting to changing dynamics. Understanding relationship phases can inform strategies for building stronger social networks, fostering cooperation, and addressing challenges that may arise in various collective settings.

Understanding these phases can help us make sense of the communication patterns and behaviours we see. It's like having a roadmap for the ups and downs of connecting with others.

Armed with these types and phases we find it easier to make sense of our relationships. It stops being a blur of emotional inputs as we start looking with intelligence and discernment.

Next, we look at some pitfalls, and the ever importance of boundaries.

Chapter 7 - Beyond the Basics: Boundaries and Pitfalls

"Good fences make good neighbours" (Robert Frost)

In the previous chapter, we learned about the importance of positive personal relationships. In this chapter, we step beyond these basics and look at the importance of boundaries as we explore some pitfalls.

Boundaries

Let's start with boundaries. The simplest definition of interpersonal boundaries is knowing and communicating what works for you and what does not. To explain the concept, let's use our skin as a metaphor for interpersonal boundaries. The skin is the physical boundary between us and the environment and can help us understand boundaries.

Our skin is like a protective shield that keeps harmful stuff out, right? Just like our skin, interpersonal boundaries protect us from harmful behaviours and attitudes from others. They're like our personal force fields.

But here's the thing, our skin can also stretch and squish a bit, just like our boundaries can be flexible depending on the situation and the relationship. It's all about finding that balance between being firm and being open.

And get this, our skin is semi-permeable, which means it lets good things in and hopefully keeps the bad stuff out. Well, our boundaries can be permeable too. They allow positive experiences and relationships to enter our lives while keeping out the negative ones.

Now, our skin is sensitive. It reacts to touch, temperature and pressure. Well, guess what? Our boundaries can be sensitive too. When someone crosses our boundaries, we can feel hurt, angry, resentful or invaded. It's important to pay attention to those feelings and communicate our boundaries clearly.

Just like our skin develops from infancy, our interpersonal boundaries develop over time. We learn from our experiences how close others are allowed to be relative to us and how close we can be towards others. It is a learning process that helps us set and maintain healthy boundaries.

And just like we take care of our skin, we need to take care of our boundaries too. That means being aware of them, communicating them clearly, and enforcing them when necessary. It also means being open to feedback and adjusting our boundaries as needed to make sure they are healthy and effective.

Navigating the complexities and maintaining healthy connections are often a challenge and we need to know how to establish boundaries. The tools we use are communication skills, self-awareness, flexibility and authenticity. With these tools, we can put the following building blocks in place.

First, being clear about expectations. It is important to express our needs and desires to others, and to be open to hearing the expectations of those around us. It is like a dance of assertiveness and clarity, where both parties understand each other's boundaries.

Setting boundaries early on in a relationship is beneficial. By doing so, we establish a strong foundation based on mutual respect and understanding. However, it is never too late. As we get to know each other more, we will realize that certain restrictions are needed to ensure a healthy dynamic.

Flexibility is another key component. We need to understand that boundaries should be clear, but we also need to recognise the importance of being open to negotiation. Sometimes, situations arise where flexibility is needed to find a balance that works for everyone involved. It is all about finding that sweet spot between firmness and adaptability.

A friend, Sarah, once shared an experience she had meditating next to a river. Sarah admired the willow tree swaying with the breeze. Its slender branches danced while the trunk stood firm and rooted.

That's how boundaries should be, she realized - firm at the core yet flexible at the edges.

She remembered being rigid before, boundaries like impenetrable walls that isolated her. Then she went too far the other way, lacking roots and swaying with every circumstance. That left her untethered.

But now Sarah found balance - steadfast in her needs yet bending when situations called for flexibility. Firm at the core like the willow's trunk, adapting at the edges like its swaying branches.

Her boundaries filtered what was unhealthy while remaining open to new perspectives for growth. Well-rooted, resilient, and in harmony with life's winds of change.

Being selective about sharing personal information is another valuable learning. Not everyone needs to know every detail of our lives. By being mindful of when, where, how, why, and with whom we share personal information, we can protect our privacy and maintain a healthy sense of boundaries. The poet Emily Dickinson said of some people, "They talk of hallowed things, aloud and embarrass my dog."

Perhaps the most important building block of interpersonal boundaries is to value our own needs and opinions. Setting boundaries means valuing ourselves and our well-being. This happens when we are willing to stand up for what we believe in and not compromise our values.

Throughout this journey, we need to embrace authenticity; embrace the power of being honest, transparent and vulnerable. We need to show up as our true selves, without fear or hesitation. By being authentic, we can establish boundaries that are true to ourselves and our values.

And just as we cannot exist without our skin, relationships cannot be healthy without boundaries. So, let us identify some common pitfalls we encounter in interpersonal relationships.

Pitfalls

There are many reasons why relationships go, as we say, pear-shaped. In my experience, the two biggest pitfalls in relationships are unmet expectations and projections.

Both have symptoms associated with them. They are like icebergs. You only see the tip made of symptoms, but underneath the surface there are many elements that build up to this. So, let's explore these major pitfalls and their symptoms. By becoming aware of them we can prevent them or mitigate the risks associated with them.

Let's start with unmet expectations.

There is nothing wrong with having expectations. Without them, life is boring. Even so, we also need to remember two important things. First, they are not laws or commands. Having an expectation does not automatically imply that they must be met. They are simply a future reality we would like to have based on our previous experiences. The second important thing we need to remember about expectations is that they are also the source of our disappointments. So, if you don't want to be disappointed, don't expect anything. Just know that you then also choose to miss out on the joy of getting what you want. The one goes with the other.

We all have expectations. Often, we are not even aware of them. Behind expectations are our needs. In the context of relationships, the need we all have is the experience of being connected. To feel we belong and that we are safe in that belonging. That we have support when needed and that we can contribute to someone else's needs. These are legitimate needs. The way we ask for these to be met and the stories we tell ourselves about how these should be met, determine whether our expectations lead to getting what we want or whether they become pitfalls that sabotage our relationships.

The biggest source of unmet expectations is the assumptions we make. Allow me to be frank. Nobody can read your mind. What you think about does not imply that others think in the same way. Please let go of this illusion. In the real world, we need to express our thoughts and expectations. This is the reason why good communication is so important.

You can express yourself according to these four points: facts, feelings, thought processes (also called the stories we tell ourselves) and expectations.

Facts are measurable realities. For example, "It is cold outside" can be measured with a thermostat. "I am feeling chilly" is the expression of my experience of the that fact. "I think I am getting a cold" is the story I tell myself about my experience, and "Please close the door" is the expectation I have of you.

Using these four points helps us to communicate clearly and prevents any assumptions from derailing the expression of our needs. Also, because communication is always a two-way street, we should listen to hear these points. Is the person sharing facts, feelings or a thought process? Is there an expectation? If it is not clear, ask.

In our family, we have a thing about apricot jam. Once, we were on a family vacation. I was in the shop and my sister-in-law phoned to ask me if there was apricot jam. I happened to be next to the shelf with apricot jam and said yes, there was apricot jam. Fast forward to the evening. My sister-in-law wanted to use apricot jam to prepare a fish to grill and asked me where the apricot jam was. I said, "It's on the shelf in the shop." She asked, "Didn't you buy it for me? I said, "No, you didn't ask me to buy it. You asked if there was apricot jam." That's an unmet expectation based on an assumption.

Some of the symptoms of unmet expectations that we experience are misunderstandings that can escalate into a conflict. Another symptom is resentment which can escalate into disgust. These are toxic in a relationship. Watch out for them.

One of the main culprits is an expectation that our partner needs to save us or solve our problems. This presents in many ways, and at its core is an external locus of control or causality, as we discussed in the chapter on autonomy.

This leads to the next big pitfall in relationships: projections. Projections are an ego-defence mechanism. Defense mechanisms are any psychological coping methods people use to protect themselves from unpleasant thoughts or feelings. Defense mechanisms shield our egos, taking off the pressure and making it easier for us to handle challenging scenarios in life.

A projection is simply the mental process by which people attribute to others what is in their minds. There are three types:

- Corresponding projection: When a person assumes that others already share their beliefs.

- Complementary projection: When someone assumes others have the same level of abilities that they do.
- Neurotic projection: When an individual assigns undesirable feelings or emotions to someone else.

When we talked about making peace with your past in the previous chapter on self-acceptance, we mentioned cognitive dissonance. This is when someone does not want to accept that they are flawed, and they project these flaws onto others. Cognitive dissonance is a perfect example of neurotic projection. Our counter for that is knowing that "nothing anybody does or says is because of you". To repeat, people say or do because of their own internal processes.

The most common symptom that shows up when we project is blame. For example, someone might say to their partner, "You make me happy or sad or angry." These are projections. Feelings cannot belong to somebody else. Our feelings are ours. Ours to experience and to take responsibility for. Sometimes it's uncomfortable and most often people are not aware that they are projecting things onto the other person.

Ego-defence mechanisms have a dark side. Let me explain by using internalised projection, also known as introjection, as an example. Introjection can be seen as the opposite of projection. Projection occurs when a person projects feelings or characteristics onto another person. Introjection occurs when a person internalises the beliefs, ideas, or voices of other people.

This behaviour is commonly associated with the internalisation of external authority. This is a natural way children start to form their perceptions as they adopt their parents' beliefs. As we saw in the unit on autonomy, part of being resilient is to step into our own authority. So, we cannot stay with introjection. The trouble with this defence mechanism is when negative traits are internalised. For example, a person believes they are a 'loser' because someone once projected their own insecurities onto them. A big part of being resilient in relationships is to check if the story that you tell yourself is your own, or whether it has been copied and pasted by someone else.

This is not an easy process. I know I am still on my journey. It makes us feel vulnerable. But here is the good news. Vulnerability is our secret weapon to becoming more resilient. Let's explore this next.

Mastering Interpersonal relationships

Having courage does not mean that we are unafraid. Having courage and showing courage means we face our fears. We are able to say, 'I have fallen, but I will get up'" (Maya Angelou)

Vulnerability

There are multitudes of misconceptions about vulnerability. Many people equate it to weakness. They are afraid that they will be taken advantage of when they admit their vulnerability. I am not going to say that this is not going to happen. The risk that we could be taken advantage of when we are vulnerable is always there. But to live is a risk, and an adventure. We can choose to look at the bicycle, knowing that we could fall, and stay where we are. Or we can climb on and go places.

I have experienced exactly the opposite of what I had often feared would happen if I displayed my vulnerable side. I was afraid of being laughed at or rejected, but instead I was embraced and accepted when I showed my vulnerability. I gained and experienced connection. In the world of Herman (that's me) vulnerability is the source of beauty. The vulnerability and innocence of a child is an evolutionary mechanism of our species expressing the need to be taken care of. As we grow older, innocence is replaced by authenticity to accompany vulnerability as the essence of beauty.

Let us clarify what vulnerability really is. My simple understanding of vulnerability is to stay present when things are uncomfortable. Our natural tendency is to check out or get away from discomfort. It is how the brain is wired. To stay present, admitting that you have no adequate response but to be in the moment. That to me is vulnerability.

It is not about spilling your guts or airing your dirty laundry in front of others – remember the Emily Dickinson quotation about embarrassing the dog? It is about being willing to be present when things are uncertain and not jumping to fix things or people. It is about taking the risk to go ahead and do the right thing even when we cannot control the outcome. It is about being honest about how we really feel and enduring the emotional exposure.

I have borrowed the following explanations from Brene Brown. Brene Brown is a researcher and author who has studied shame, vulnerability and human connection for over twenty years. She defines vulnerability as "uncertainty, risk, and emotional exposure. But vulnerability is not weakness; it's our most accurate measure of courage."[xvi]

Her work emphasizes the importance of positive interpersonal relationships which she defines as those that are built on authenticity, vulnerability and empathy. We can summarize Brown's understanding as follows:

1. Authenticity: Positive interpersonal relationships require authenticity, which means being true to oneself and others. Authenticity involves being honest, transparent and vulnerable, and it requires the courage to show up as one's true self.

2. Vulnerability: Vulnerability is essential for positive interpersonal relationships. This involves taking emotional risks and being willing to share one's feelings, thoughts and experiences. It requires the courage to be imperfect and to embrace one's flaws and weaknesses.

3. Empathy: Empathy involves understanding and sharing the feelings of others, and requires active listening, perspective-taking and emotional intelligence.

4. Connection: Positive interpersonal relationships are built on a foundation of connection, which involves a sense of belonging, acceptance and mutual support. Connection requires the willingness to be vulnerable and authentic, and it involves a deep sense of trust and respect.

At first, this sounds scary. Well, to be honest, it is always scary to be vulnerable. But the rewards I have gained in my relationships after being authentic and vulnerable motivate me to do it again. The risk/ reward ratio is not equal. The reward outweighs the risk by far. Try it. It will make you more resilient.

You are the common ground

Have you noticed something peculiar? In all these points surrounding positive relationships, there is one constant. You. You are the common ground. You are the starting point, the center and the endpoint of the relationship labyrinth.

People are in essence mirrors of each other. I mirror my partner's life to her and my partner mirrors my life back to me. If we start thinking about that in relationships, we understand the saying "What you say about other people says more about you than about them" because you are mirroring or projecting what's inside you onto other people.

So, listen to yourself when you talk about other people. Whenever you say something negative about somebody it's probably because there is a negative element you recognise in yourself, but you are uncomfortable with it, like most people. Here we should be careful that we do not fall into cognitive dissonance – when we don't want to accept the story that we are a flawed person. And so we project that flaw onto other people. This is not an effective strategy. For the flaw does not go away if it is in you. Better to deal with it with empathy and kindness.

The surprising twist in the tale is that the opposite is also true. When we see something beautiful in somebody else, we can only recognise that beauty because that beauty is in us as well. As the mystic Rumi puts it, "The beauty you see in me is a reflection of you." Is this not powerful! We need to take responsibility and ownership for projecting the positive, just like we take responsibility and ownership for the projection of bad things. By doing this, we become whole again.

And this process of taking ownership is a challenge. First, because it's uncomfortable. It makes me uncomfortable to realize that I can't blame anybody else anymore. I am responsible for my own well-being.

Conclusion

That was a mouthful. Let's summarize. Positive interpersonal relationships are essential for our well-being as they directly touch on a core human need to belong.

We acknowledge that interpersonal relationships can be as complex as wandering through a labyrinth. And it helps to know a labyrinth has a start and an end. It helps to know that relationships go through phases and that there are different types of relationships.

Building positive relationships includes having healthy boundaries and being on the lookout for the pitfalls of unrealistic expectations and projections. It also asks for us to be brave enough to be vulnerable.

And as the labyrinth teaches us, it all circles back to our relationship with ourselves. We are the common denominator in all our relationships. It therefore starts and ends with having a positive relationship with ourselves.

"Our greatest glory is not in never falling, but in rising every time we fall." (Confucius)

Part 4 – Mastering Your Environment

"The ecologist has a much more comprehensive and holistic view of the world. We're looking at the natural environment as well as the human-built environment and the connectivity between the two - how do the natural environment and the human-built environment interact and interface with each other" (Ken Yeang)

Chapter 8 – The Main Issue

Introduction

Our environment plays a significant role in our well-being.

Neuroscience research has established that there is a strong connection between architectural design, human emotions, behaviour and well-being, emphasizing that buildings and cities can affect our mood and well-being because specialized cells in the brain are attuned to the geometry and arrangement of the spaces we live in.

Additionally, the architecture of buildings can impact cognitive function using sound, with acoustically friendly buildings helping to reduce stress and improve cognitive function.

The arrangement of structures and colours used in interior design have also been shown to have a significant impact on how people generate a feeling of place and how they react to it. An everyday example of this is when we walk into a restaurant or a bar. We will tell people it has a welcoming atmosphere, or it feels a bit dodgy.

Architecture as an influencer

Some examples of buildings that have been designed to evoke specific emotions include:

The iconic Sagrada Familia, a basilica in Barcelona, Spain, is known for its awe-inspiring and emotionally evocative design, aiming to create a sense of wonder and spiritual reverence.

Then there is the architecture of the Topkapi Palace in Istanbul, Turkey. It was designed to evoke specific emotions and reflect the power, wealth and status of the Ottoman Empire.

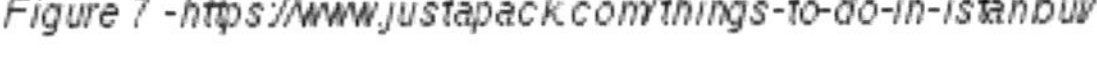

Figure 7 -https://www.justapack.com/things-to-do-in-istanbul/

The architecture of the palace (a mix of Byzantine, Ottoman and Islamic styles) was meant to exude majesty and prestige. The grand domes, ornate carvings and intricate tile work that adorn the palace interiors and exteriors were all intended to convey a sense of grandeur and importance.

The grandeur and size of the palace showcased the power and authority of the Ottoman sultans. Its imposing structure and ornate details such as the intricate tile work and carved stone were designed to impress visitors and reinforce the ruler's strength and dominance. The palace gardens, reflecting the Ottoman love of nature, provided a serene and relaxing environment for the sultan and his court. Terraces, arranged in rows of cypresses stretching to many parts of the palace complex and along the seashore, evoked a sense of peace and tranquillity. The use of geometrical designs in the flower and vegetable beds and the fountains and pools express the Islamic tradition of harmony with nature and a balance of aesthetics.

Our environment does not consist only of architecture and its influences on us. It includes the social, political and economic dimensions of our life. A big part of being emotionally resilient is having the ability to manage and flourish in our unique environments.

The ultimate objective

This whole course builds up to this objective: the ability to manage our lives effectively in the surrounding world.

I assume that persons who possess a feeling of mastery and capability in handling their environment achieve a high level of competency. They have control over a wide range of complex external activities, utilize surrounding opportunities effectively, and can select or create environments that align with their personal needs and values.

In contrast, low competency is characterized by difficulties in managing everyday affairs, a sense of being unable to change or improve the surrounding context, unawareness of opportunities available in the surroundings, and a lack of control over the external world.

The story of the two sisters illustrates the point. One becomes a sought-after therapist with a happy family and friends; the other an alcoholic on the streets. When asked why they are as they are, they both give the same reason. "My mother was an alcoholic."

If this is our departure point, let us look at what we can do about it in today's fast-paced and ever-changing world.

Individuals face demanding challenges. These challenges include navigating the intricacies of the global economy in our day-to-day living on a high level, or a simple relationship challenge in the family.

The demands of the information society we live in require not only technical skills but also a mastery of sociocultural tools for effective interaction.

In this unit, we focus on two of these sociocultural tools and how they assist us in being emotionally resilient. This asks for more than a blend of knowledge and skills; it's the ability to meet complex demands by mobilizing resources, including skills and attitudes in specific contexts. For instance, effective communication draws on language knowledge, practical IT skills, and attitudes towards the audience.

We need more than just having access to them; individuals must also develop the necessary skills and attitudes to use them appropriately. This process involves creating and adapting knowledge and skills, making the tools active participants in an individual's engagement with their environment. This ability plays a significant role in navigating through the diverse circumstances we face.

We can categorize these sociocultural tools into three main types: cognitive, socio-cultural, and physical tools.

1. **Cognitive tools**: These are mental resources that help individuals process information, solve problems, and make decisions. They include skills, knowledge and attitudes that enable people to interact with their environment and adapt to new situations. We used some of these tools when we talked about how the stories we tell ourselves influence our self-acceptance as well as how to be more autonomous in executing our personal authority.

2. **Socio-cultural tools**: We use these to interact with others and understand their social context. They include language, communication styles and cultural norms that shape how people relate to one another and navigate their environment. We touched on this when we explored positive relationships. We will further explore the tool of effective communication in one of the following chapters.

3. **Physical tools**: These are the tangible objects individuals use to accomplish tasks and achieve their goals. They can range from simple

objects like pens and pencils to more complex tools like computers and smartphones that enable people to access information and communicate.

We focus on the first two – cognitive and socio-cultural tools. Under cognitive tools, we explore how to be change-fit in an ever-changing environment. While in socio-cultural type tools, we focus on effective communication. Physical tools fall outside the scope of this book as each unique situation asks for its corresponding tool. And I am sure you know better than I do what you will need in your specific context.

In the next chapter, we begin with effective communication.

Chapter 9 – Effective Communication

Jack and Max are walking back from a religious service. Jack wonders whether it would be all right to smoke while praying.

Max replies, "Why don't you ask the priest?"

So, Jack goes up to the priest and asks, "Father, may I smoke while I pray?"

But the priest says, "No, my son, you may not. That's disrespectful to our religion."

Jack goes back to his friend and tells him what the good priest told him.

Max says, "I'm not surprised. You asked the wrong question. Let me try."

And so Max goes up to the priest and asks, "Father, may I pray while I smoke?" to which he eagerly replies, "By all means, my son. By all means."

It is not always what you say but the way you say it that determines what you get.

Framework of communication

Let's start with the basics by looking at the communication framework.

Aristotle explained oral communication as a process composed of a speaker, a message and a listener. He points out that the person at the end of the communication process, the listener, holds the key to whether or not communication takes place.

Harold Lasswell, a political scientist, formulated the main elements of communication: Who says what in which channel to whom with what effect. The point Lasswell adds is that **there must be an "effect" if communication is to take place**. If we have communicated, we've "motivated" or produced an effect.

The Shannon and Weaver communication model adds noise to the communication process. Noise, Weaver said, "may be distortions of sound (in telephony, for example) or static (in radio), or distortions in shape or shading of picture (television), or errors in transmission (telegraph or facsimile), etc."

The "noise" concept introduced by Shannon and Weaver can be used to illustrate semantic noise that interferes with communication. Semantic noise is the problem connected with differences in meaning that people assign to words, to voice inflexions in speech, to gestures and expressions, and other similar noise in writing.

I simplify this by distinguishing between external and internal noise. External noise is a radio playing in the background. Internal noise is semantic noise. All the preconceived conceptions or emotions we have around the speaker, the message, and the expected effect.

Semantic noise is a more serious problem or barrier to developing effective communication than most realize. It is hard to detect that semantic noise has interfered with communication. Too often the person sending a message chooses to use words and phrases that have a certain meaning to him or her. However, they may have an altogether different meaning to individuals receiving the message.

Semantic or internal noise can be understood as the biases we all have that prevent us from communicating effectively or hearing properly. A variety of biases influence how individuals perceive and respond to messages. Here are five common biases relevant to interpersonal communication:

Confirmation bias - The tendency to seek, interpret and remember information that confirms preexisting beliefs or values. In interpersonal communication, individuals may selectively attend to information that supports their existing opinions and dismiss or downplay information that challenges those beliefs.

Stereotyping bias - Making assumptions or generalisations about a person or group based on their perceived characteristics or stereotypes rather than assessing them as unique individuals. Stereotyping can lead to misinterpretations and miscommunications, as individuals may be judged based on preconceived notions rather than their actual thoughts, feelings or behaviours.

The Halo effect - Forming a general impression of a person based on a single positive or negative trait or characteristic. The halo effect can lead to biased perceptions, as individuals may extend their evaluation of one aspect of a person to influence their overall judgement, potentially overlooking other relevant information.

Self-Serving bias - The tendency to attribute positive events to one's own character or abilities while attributing negative events to external factors. In interpersonal communication, individuals may take credit for successes but blame external factors for failures, affecting how they communicate and respond to feedback.

Cultural bias - The tendency to interpret and judge behaviour and communication based on one's own cultural norms and values. We all know people who work internationally from home across different cultures. Being aware of this bias is especially important today. Cultural biases can lead to misunderstandings and miscommunications, especially in diverse and multicultural settings, where individuals may interpret messages differently based on their cultural backgrounds.

Being aware of these biases is crucial for effective interpersonal communication, as it allows individuals to approach conversations with a more open mind and a better understanding of potential sources of miscommunication.

In the interest of good communication, we need to work to hold semantic noise to the lowest level possible.

Building blocks of effective communication

One way to minimize semantic noise is to send and listen for a whole message. A whole message consists of: Facts, Feelings, Thoughts and Expectations.

For example, when I ask you to please close the door, you know my expectation of you is to act by closing the door. If I add, "It is cold outside, please close the door," you now have a measurable fact to add to the message. We can take the thermostat outside and determine the temperature. If I add, "It is cold outside. I am not feeling well; I think I am getting a cold. Please close the door," I have added feelings and thoughts to the message. This is a whole message and there is a minimal chance of a misunderstanding.

So, take some time to prepare your messages. It saves trouble further down the line. At the same time, when you listen to someone, ask yourself whether this person is sharing facts, feelings, or just expectations? Or maybe just their thoughts? If the message is incomplete, ask for clarity around the missing elements of the whole message.

Let's dive deeper into each of these four elements as both listener and speaker.

Facts – observation vs interpretation vs judgement

When sharing facts, it helps to distinguish between observation, interpretation, and judgement.

Observation is a neutral act of gathering information, based on visible behaviour or events. Observations are objective and evoke learning. They are also called awareness or mindfulness.

Interpretation deals with spoken language in real time. Interpretation is primarily a communication process that helps people make sense of and understand more about the received message.

Judgement is a subjective opinion about the relative value or merit of an observation. Judgements are formed by comparing "what is" to "what should be" and assigning a label of good or bad.

The major difference between observation and judgement is that observation is only taking note of what we perceive with our senses and doesn't involve any kind of evaluation. Judgement involves evaluation of some kind. For example:

- Observation: that man is wearing a blue shirt

- Evaluation: that shirt is ugly
- Judgement: that man lacks fashion sense

When we observe someone or something, we are watching or hearing them without forming an opinion or commenting on their actions, dress, speech, etc.

When we judge someone or something, we are observing and forming an opinion. Meaning we either support or dislike what they are saying, how they're acting, or possibly what they are wearing. When we openly comment about right or wrong we are judging. Once I judge someone it may play a pivotal role as to whether they become a friend. Or it returns to the place of either liked or disliked, a matter of personal opinion which holds no relevance.

When sending or receiving a message, make sure that you are sending the facts not your interpretations or judgements.

Feelings – non-verbal/micro-expressions, projections

Feelings or experiences make up the bulk of all communication. Only about eight percent of any message is verbal. The rest is non-verbal. Non-verbal includes things like body posture, micro-expressions, volume and tone of voice.

Here are several types of non-verbal communication with brief explanations and examples:

Body language involves the use of facial expressions, gestures, posture and movements to convey messages. For example, a person leaning forward during a presentation can signal interest and engagement.

Some of the lesser-known non-verbal cues are: proximity, touch, paralinguistics and artefacts.

Proximity refers to the physical distance between individuals, which can convey intimacy or formality.

Touch involves physical contact, conveying emotions such as warmth, empathy or authority. For example, a pat on the back to show support or a handshake to convey trust and agreement.

Paralinguistics involves variations in pitch, tone, volume and speed of speech to convey meaning. For example, a cheerful tone can convey enthusiasm, while a soft voice might indicate sympathy.

Artefacts refer to objects or accessories that convey information about a person's identity or status. For example, wearing a wedding ring can communicate marital status.

There is much material available on non-verbal communication. If you are interested, I suggest you do a Google search. One important thing I need to emphasize is the wholeness of a message. Especially when it comes to non-verbal messages. Do not jump on one cue only. Keep the context in mind. Someone standing with their arms folded in front of them might just be cold and not necessarily defensive.

When it comes to communicating feelings, things tend to get messy. Few people have the skill to communicate their emotional experiences effectively. Two researched topics help untangle this dimension of a message.

The first is the existence of mirror neurons. Neuroscience has identified a class of neurons responsible for learning, called mirror neurons.[xvii] The idea is that thanks to mirror neurons, we can first observe an action (what is being done?), then understand the intention of that action (why is it happening?) and finally, reproduce the same action to achieve similar results (the motor component).

Both our understanding of an action and the ability to then mirror that same action are of great significance to learning, speech perception and emotional intelligence. One argument is that since mirror neurons are responsible for both the "what" and the "what for" of a particular action, they are strongly linked to our ability to show empathy.[xviii]

Empathy is the ability to understand and share the feelings of another person. It involves being able to perceive and comprehend the emotions, perspectives and experiences of others, and to respond with sensitivity and compassion. Empathy goes beyond simply recognizing someone else's emotions; it also involves the capacity to connect with those feelings on a deeper level.

This is good for communicating effectively. Just watch out for the internalisation of the feelings. When we observe someone being sad, we feel sadness as well, because we empathise with them. Please note that we have empathy, not sadness. The sadness belongs to the observed person. We can relate because the sad behaviour resonates with our own experiences of sadness, but we do not feel the same sadness in the same way.

Someone's lived experience is theirs. Let us be respectful and distinguish between what belongs to us and what belongs to others. As seen previously, it is unfair to project our stuff onto other people so let us not diminish their experience by adding our memory of a similar experience. It is way better to just acknowledge the experience. This way, they feel seen or heard. Just listening is enough. We do not need to fix anything, or worse deny the experience by minimizing it. I heard of someone whose child died. One person responded, "Well, at least you have two other children left."

The second field of research is around the identification of the four core emotions: Love, fear, anger and sadness. Each one of these emotions has an evolutionary status. In other words, they have established themselves through millenniums of evolutionary trials and errors as the main emotions in our system. Therefore, when someone is expressing their emotions it is safe to ask ourselves whether they are expressing anger, fear, sadness or love.

Yes, sometimes things get messy when, for example, fear is expressed as anger. So, it is always better to check in by asking. Are you angry or afraid? And when the answer is given, respond with empathy.

Thoughts – argument logic, biases

Communicating our thoughts might sound straightforward. I am just verbalizing my thinking. This is true, yet at the same time, few of us are thinking effectively. Most of us think regurgitatively. With respect to the reader, most of us, myself included, think pre-thought thoughts. And we repeat them often.

A good example of this is the meme culture we are all used to. "A picture is worth a thousand words, but a meme is worth a thousand thoughts," said Aditya Shukla, while forwarding memes to different people.[xix]

• • • •

Richard Dawkins, a pioneering evolutionary biologist and author of *The Selfish Gene*, coined the term "meme," which is a social gene. Like genetics, he conceptualised memetics, the spread of ideas from people to people that are not inherited like genes but spread like a virus, socially. So, we say, "It went viral; it's a meme." While genes typically spread vertically and replicate through inheritance, memes spread and replicate horizontally and vertically. Memes become copies of ideas that spread through people, like culture.[xx]

This is not a big deal until we want to communicate effectively. Then it helps if we logically order our thoughts.

Logical thinking can be defined as the act of analyzing a situation and coming up with a sensible solution. It plays a crucial role in effective communication, as it helps us organise our thoughts coherently, present arguments logically, and convey ideas clearly and in a structure. Let us explore this further.

What is the deal with logical thinking? Imagine making decisions without the drama, and solving problems like a pro. Some of the benefits of logical thinking are that it helps you solve problems by breaking down big stuff into bite-sized pieces and conquer like a boss. It helps us to make smart decisions. It helps you weigh options, predict outcomes and make decisions that make sense. Importantly, it makes our communication strong. Logical thinkers communicate in a way that everyone gets. No confusion, just clarity.

There are three main types of logical thinking:

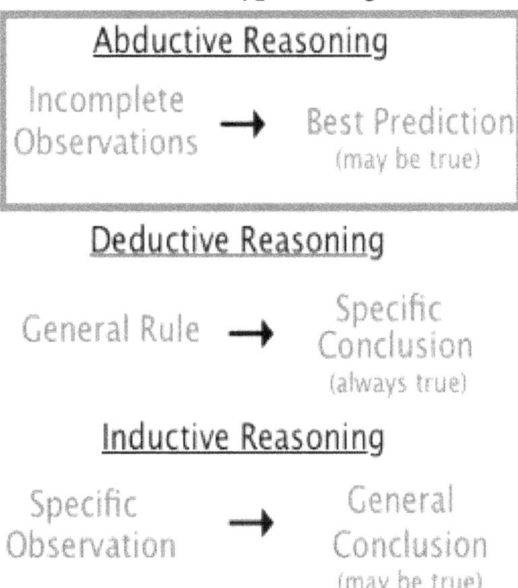

• • • •

The first is deductive thinking. This is when we start with the big picture, break it down, and unveil specific answers. Deductive reasoning, or *deduction*, is making an inference based on widely accepted facts or premises. If a beverage is defined as "drinkable through a straw", one could use deduction to determine soup to be a beverage.

The second is inductive thinking. This is when we gather details, make general conclusions, and feel the satisfaction of being pretty darn sure about things. Inductive reasoning, or *induction*, is making an inference based on an observation, often of a sample. You can induce that the soup is tasty if you observe all of your friends consuming it and asking for more.

The third type is abductive thinking. This is when we form the best theories based on what's in front of us. Abductive reasoning, or *abduction*, is making a probable conclusion from what you know. If you see an abandoned bowl of hot soup on the table, you can use abduction to conclude the owner of the soup is likely to return soon. Or they didn't enjoy the taste.

Here is another way to think about these types:[xxi]

- Deductive reasoning: a conclusion guaranteed
- Inductive reasoning: a conclusion merely likely
- Abductive reasoning: taking your best shot.

When communicating your logic, never assume people know what you know. Often when we work through a problem, we only share the solution. But the solution is the tip of the iceberg and underneath the surface, we did all the logical thinking work. Made assumptions, tested them (hopefully) and came to conclusions. If you want to communicate your thoughts effectively, take people with you through the journey. Step by step. Don't bore them with the petty details, just let them follow your process.

Of course, not every communication event needs to follow all the steps listed. No, rather weave them into a conversation. Dumping your facts, feelings, thoughts and expectations all in one monologue will guarantee you a blank stare of incomprehension. See communication more like a dance, or a game of tennis. Each partner offers each other variations based on all four communication movements.

Much has to do with timing too. It does not help to respond logically to an emotional outburst. Empathy first then logical later.

Expectations – know what you want, and say it clearly

The last element of a whole message is to communicate your expectations to the listener.

On a superficial and task-orientated level, it is easier to communicate what we want. Whether it is asking for a report or a simple action like closing the door. Logical thinking can help us to crystallize these expectations. Remember to check your assumptions around prior shared knowledge. Do not assume people know what you know.

The challenge is we are not always aware of what we want when it comes to more personal needs. Our deeper needs tend to present themselves as symptoms. For example, someone who might be afraid will present their need for safety in an angry, combative style. The flipside could also present itself when such a person fakes boredom and disengages.

I do not have the space in this story to go into the deeper psychological processes that drive this behaviour. So, for our conversation regarding effective communication, I will share five of the most basic needs: a sense of safety, a sense of belonging, the experience of value, autonomy and fairness.

Being and feeling *safe* is possibly the deepest need we all share. We feel safe when we know what will happen next is not dangerous. Safety determines our existence, and whenever we feel threatened, our bodies are programmed to respond with fear. Fear can present itself either in a fight, flight or freeze response. So, when someone comes at you with an aggressive demeanour, it might be that they are just afraid. Someone else might present their fear through avoidance behaviour while someone might just ignore the issue and do nothing.

In communication, when you feel unsafe, identify what the threat is and address this issue. It is easier to ask someone to deal with an identified issue than to wonder what the symptomatic issues refer to. An example of this could be when your partner starts fighting with you about taking the wrong route. You can respond by fighting back or shutting down (fight or flight) or you can stay curious and explore what the fear behind being lost is.

We also addressed the experience of *value*, or, expressed differently, the experience of status when we talked about the natural social hierarchy that exists. When communicating with someone, be aware of this process and check whether what is said sounds condescending or not. It is better to be appreciative of the person with whom you are communicating. This will give them the experience of being valued and they will open their minds to what you want to communicate.

The perception of *fairness* has much to do with observed behaviour, even if it is secondhand observation. For us to be better communicators regarding fairness, it helps to remember the pitfall of attribution bias we discussed in Chapter 3. To refresh your memory, attribution bias is a shortcut our brains take when attributing a reason for someone's behaviour. The bias is that we attribute personal character flaws to someone's behaviour rather than keeping the context in mind. And we tend to do the opposite when we explain our own behaviour. Here it is helpful to remember Hanlon's razor which states rather assume incompetence than malice, as this story illustrates:

One day a man runs up to Socrates and says: "I have to tell you something about your friend who…" Socrates interrupts him. "Hold on. About the story you're about to tell me, did you put it through the three sieves?"

The man was not familiar with the three sieves, so Socrates continued: "The first is the sieve of truth. Are you sure that what you are going to tell me is true?"

"To tell the truth," said the man, "No, I just overheard it."

"What about the sieve of goodness or kindness? Will you tell me something good or positive about this man?"

The man shook his head.

"Now, what about the last sieve? Is it necessary to tell me what you're so excited about?"

The man bowed his head in shame.

Socrates smiled and said, "Well, if the story you're about to tell me is neither true, good or necessary, just forget it and don't bother me with it."

Lastly, respect *boundaries* in communicating your expectations. You have the fullest right to express your needs or wants. At the same time, the listener has the fullest right to agree to or not to fulfil these expectations. And you need to be okay with this. There is no guarantee that your expectations will be met. Especially not in the way you envisioned it. It is a good habit to let go of the consequences of your expressed expectations.

Once words leave your mouth, you no longer have control over them. So, speak your truth boldly and wisely. And if the person you are speaking to is important enough to you, be willing to be present and vulnerable. The connection with someone you love is more important than being right.

Chapter 10 – Being Change-Fit

"Sometimes good things fall apart so better things could fall together"
(Marilyn Monroe)

• • • •

"Life is flux," said the Greek philosopher Heraclitus (circa 500 BC.) Everything is constantly shifting, and becoming something other than what it was before. Like a river, life flows ever onwards, and while we may step from the riverbank into the river, the waters flowing over our feet will never be the same waters that flowed even one moment before. Heraclitus concluded that since the very nature of life is change, to resist this natural flow was to resist the very essence of our existence. "There is nothing permanent except change," he said.

And because this is true, one of the key skills we all need to be competent in is to be "change-fit."

To be fit refers to the ability to carry out daily tasks with energy and alertness, without too much tiredness and with plenty of energy to enjoy the good things in life and to meet unforeseen challenges. It does not mean you do not get tired. It means it takes longer for you to get tired and when you do get tired and rest, the recovery time is shorter than when you are unfit. You get back in the game more quickly.

Change-fit, then refers to your "bounce back" rate to deal with life in flux.

The philosophy and thinking of Heraclitus influenced the Stoic philosophers.[1] The Stoics believed the natural world is made up of a series of processes that are changing, but "if we want to live happily with nature, we [must] live in harmony with it." The Stoics advised appreciating things now but also understanding that they are not forever.

Stoicism argues that we should not resist change but face up to it. "The question is, do we change with it?" says Sellars.[xxii] "Stoics say we don't have any choice, we can't fight it." Now, that is easier said than done. I found in my own life, that although I love and embrace diversity, I struggle with real change. A few years ago, we moved to another country after living in the same city for thirty years. Man, was it hard!

Julia Samuel, a British psychotherapist and paediatric counsellor, echoes my experience when she says "Change is the one certainty of life, and pain is the agent of change; it forces you to wake up and see the world differently, and the discomfort of it forces you to see the reality of it. It's through pain that we learn, personally and universally."

Accepting change also makes you better at it, she says. "It's the paradox that the more you allow yourself to accept that change is bound to happen, the more likely you are to change intentionally and adapt." Change can be an engine of progress.

Virginia Woolf, the writer, puts it beautifully: "A self that goes on changing is a self that goes on living." Or in the words of Octavia E Butler, an American science fiction author, "All that you touch, you change. All that you change, changes you. The only lasting truth is change." This is not a call to resign to fate, it is a call to take responsibility for the shifting patterns of one's world."

The essayist Maria Popova reminds us that to be human is to suffer from a peculiar inherited blindness: "In the face of any great change, we can see with terrifying clarity the familiar firm footing we stand to lose. At the same time, we fill the void of the unfamiliar before us with dread at the potential loss rather than joy over the potential gain of gladness and gratification. We fail to envision the gains of change because we haven't yet experienced them. "[xxiii]

Psychologist Daniel Gilbert reminds us that "human beings are works in progress that mistakenly think they are finished."

We therefore need to adapt the story we tell ourselves about change. In this chapter, we reconnect with our progress in becoming change-fit.

To help us adapt our story about change, let us first look at the research done on change. We explore three of the many models of change – cyclical, linear and systemic. Models, especially thinking models, helps us make sense of our world. With it, we give structure to our stories and by doing this, we can tell more useful stories.

The three models we will explore act as three possible background stories we can use. It is like a marathon runner who researches the ups and downs of the route before running. Once we have a background picture, we look at the change process and what we could do to deal with it. Lastly, we look at some practical exercises each one of us can do to become change fit.

Models of change – cyclical model

The first model of change I call the cyclical model, or the flow of change. Change is a continuous process that comes and goes and comes again. Think of the river Heraclitus talked about. It continuously flows to the sea, where it evaporates to form clouds that rain on the mountains to flow in rivers back to the sea.

Figure 8- Image by lcallard210 from Pixabay

Arnold Toynbee's *A Study of History,* based on exhaustive studies of some thirty civilizations, suggests that the beginning of civilization (civilization being an ordered co-habitation) consists of a transition from a static condition to one of dynamic activity. Toynbee saw the birth of civilizations as the result of a dynamic interplay which he called a "challenge-and-response" process.

A challenge from the natural or social environment provokes a creative response in a society or a social group, which convinces that society to enter the process of civilization. Civilization then continues to grow when it successfully responds to the initial challenge. This growth generates cultural momentum that carries the society beyond a state of equilibrium into an overbalance that presents itself as a fresh challenge. In this way, the initial pattern of challenge-and-response is repeated in successive phases of growth, each successful response producing a disequilibrium that requires new creative adjustments.

An interesting and real-world example of this is the hundredth monkey effect. The hundredth monkey phenomenon dates back to a study in 1952 that followed the behaviour of a hungry young female monkey living in the wild on a Japanese island. One day, perhaps fed up with the residual taste of grit in her mouth after mealtimes, she had a bright idea. She washed her dirt-encrusted potatoes in a stream before eating them. Her family watched on curiously and then followed suit. Then her playmates and then their families. One-by-one, this behavioural change spread within the troop.

But it was what scientists reportedly observed next that was remarkable. By the time the 100th monkey got involved (yes, I agree, it's a suspiciously round number) the new idea transformed from being an exception to the norm. Overnight, every monkey and every troop on the whole island began washing their potatoes before eating them.

The hundredth monkey is now described as the point at which 'critical mass' is reached – the tipping point for all other monkeys to follow suit.

It's an interesting tale that caught our eye. Not because of an obsession with monkeys or potatoes. But because critical mass theory can be considered in light of every social movement, big and small.

Models of change – linear model

The alternative to this model is the linear or evolutionary view. Herbert Spencer, the British philosopher and sociologist who coined the phrase "survival of the fittest" (often misattributed to Charles Darwin), saw all social change as the expression of a natural law of progress. The dynamic force in progress was, like that in biological evolution, the competitive struggle for existence in which the fit survive and the unfit perish. An example of this would be the competition in some businesses. Take Blockbuster, the video rental company. At its peak,

Blockbuster had thousands of stores and was the go-to place for movie rentals. However, with the rise of digital streaming services like Netflix, Blockbuster failed to adapt its business model to the changing landscape of media consumption. It did not invest in an online platform early enough and ultimately went out of business.[xxiv]

Another influencer of this view of change is Karl Marx. He claimed that all changes in society arise from the development of its internal contradictions. Internal contradictions are embodied in society's classes and present themselves as a class struggle because of their oppositional interaction. Class struggle was the driving force of history for Marx. He held that all important historical progress was born in conflict, struggle, and violent revolution. Human suffering and sacrifice were a necessary price paid for social change.

Marx's theories were based on Hegel's view of history as an opposite point of view progression. Hegel claimed that one concept (thesis) inevitably generates its opposite (antithesis) and that their interaction leads to a new concept (synthesis), which in turn becomes the thesis of a new triad.

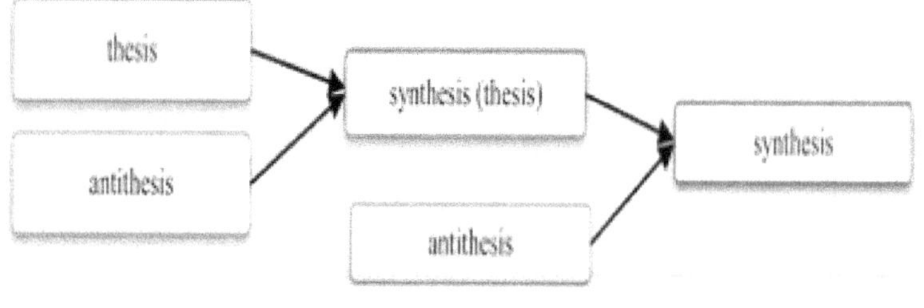

· · · ·

And so, change continues.

I believe that this model is limiting. It is based on a skewed and simplified assumption of evolution. Survival of the fittest is a small element in the whole process of evolution. It also includes collaboration and experimentation and therefore I think it is better to call this model of change a linear model.

Models of change – systemic model

The third change model embraces a systemic view of the world. This model is probably the most difficult to get a grip on, but once we do, life is made in a beautiful way. Life is too complex to limit it to a linear cause-and-effect reasoning. The systemic model takes as a departure point that everything is interconnected and therefore any one of those connections can initiate change.

The study of complex systems has pioneered a new approach to understanding the instability and fluctuations that characterize seemingly random events, be it at the level of molecules, biological systems, or even social systems.

The central discovery of the theory of dynamic systems is the commonness of instability. In essence, instability means that small changes in initial conditions may lead to large amplifications of the effects of the changes. It's like a stone dropped in a pond that sends ripples to the edges.

In his book *Order Out of Chaos,* Ilya Prigogine explores the nature of change in what he calls "dissipative (the process of gradually disappearing or losing energy, for example, by cooling down) structures."[xxv] Dissipative structures are best described as "open" systems in the sense that they interact with the larger world around them by constantly trading energy and maintaining themselves through an endless dynamic flow.

One of the chief characteristics of these systems is that they are subject to constant fluctuations that allow for novelty and unpredictable change. A single fluctuation, adding its strength to other fluctuations, may become powerful enough to reorganise the whole system into a new pattern.

The points at which this happens are "bifurcation (split, branching, division) points" at which deterministic description breaks down, and the system follows one of several possible forks in the road.[xxvi]

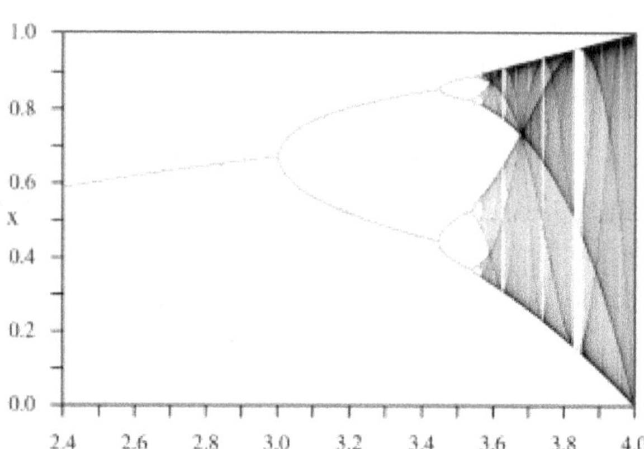

These "unpredictable" processes demonstrate that open systems are not mechanistic but random. Prigogine uses the term randomness to denote not blind chance, but rather non-determinism, spontaneity and novelty. Open systems can thus be thought of as dynamic and creative. In contrast to systems at equilibrium in which no further exchanges take place, open systems are constantly attuned to their environments.

In these open systems, stuff is not isolated and solitary, as scientists once assumed. Instead, it is responsive, relational and self-adapting in response to the activities of others.

I like this approach to change. Is it not better to think of the change that is happening as a creative process than resisting it because we fear the loss of what is known?

There is growing evidence that systemic change is not a mechanistic, progressive and linear phenomenon whose causes and effects can be isolated. Nature appears more like a complicated web of relations between various parts of a unified whole. The German quantum physicist Werner Heisenberg put it this way: "The world thus appears as a complicated tissue of events, in which connections of different kinds alternate or overlap or combine and thereby determine the texture of the whole." And the poet Rumi reminds us, "You are not a drop in the ocean, you are the entire ocean in a drop."

In complex societies under stress (like we are experiencing) there are usually many revitalisation movements competing for attention and converts as the culture begins to disintegrate. The change process begins with a shift away from cultural harmony, a change that shows up first in the form of increased individual stress. A growing number of individuals find that they are unable to meet certain cultural expectations.

An example of this is the women's rights movement.[xxvii] In the aftermath of World War II, the lives of women in developed countries changed dramatically. Household technology eased the burdens of homemaking, life expectancies increased dramatically, and the growth of the service sector opened up thousands of jobs not dependent on physical strength. Despite these socioeconomic transformations, cultural attitudes (especially concerning women's work) and legal precedents still reinforced sexual inequalities. The women's movement worked to overturn laws that enforced discrimination, broaden women's self-awareness, and challenge traditional stereotypes of women as passive, dependent or irrational. While the movement's peak is often associated with the 1960s and 70s, organised activism on behalf of women has continued through the third and fourth waves of feminism into the early 21st century. Today, even though a lot of ground is still to be covered, women are accepted as equal partners by the majority of society.

At first, this is perceived by both the individual and society at large as an individual problem. But as the number of these individual deviations grows, it begins to weaken the social fabric, eventually to the point where society must acknowledge that the problem is more than personal. At this stage, it is difficult for society to return to a state of equilibrium without undergoing a process of revitalisation.

An example of this is the story of Galileo. Galileo's observations discredited the Aristotelian theory of an earth-centred solar system in favour of the Copernican heliocentric model (that the earth orbited the sun).[xxviii] He backed up his theory with evidence from many years of hard research. Galileo laid the pathway for modern science and astronomy to improve and develop. Today we accept this as a truth no one questions.

Of the three models discussed, the first and the third resonate the most with me. The first makes intuitive sense, and the third, even though it is the most difficult to understand, is the closest to reality. The second model is easy to understand. It works like a pendulum. But life is too beautifully complex to be reduced to a tick-tock rhythm.

Now that we know the background music to our change-fit story, let's look at the next building block, the change process. I hope that when you understand this process, you will have anchor points to which you can bind your change story.

The change processes

Because none of us are immune to change, it helps to know what to expect. A change process assists us in this when it tries to explain the different phases a change process will go through. There are many such change processes out there, and I take my cue from Bruce Fuller at the Berkeley School of Education.[xxix] He breaks down the process into three main parts: the long goodbye, the messy middle and the new beginnings.

We look at each one of these in more detail:

The long goodbye

The long goodbye is generally the first phase. Daryl Conner, author of *Managing at the Speed of Change,* calls it the preparation phase. This long goodbye starts with pre-contemplation. As we have seen in the systemic model of change, the shift from harmony happens gradually with individuals experiencing discomfort with the status quo, while the rest of society enjoys their ignorance. The handful of individuals that feel discomfort, start to evaluate their behaviour. Explore what they want as an alternative to this discomfort, and start to explain and personalize the risk to address the discomfort.

An old preacher said, "People don't change when they see the light. They change when they feel the heat." The fable about the frog in the pot explains this well.

The frog is caught in the pond, brought into the kitchen and placed in a pot of cold water. The frog experiences disharmony. This is not the pond it knows, but the water is clean and interesting things are moving about and he can see flies buzzing around.

Next, nothing happens. Pre-contemplation just moves to contemplation. Individuals are still contemplating the discomfort. Yet, it isn't too bad and maybe it will go away, and if not, we can deal with it in the future. Maybe someone somewhere will do something.

Our frog is now on the stove and there is a slow-burning fire under the pot. The frog feels it but finds it relaxing and wonders why he was not in this hot spring earlier.

This contemplation phase will go on for as long as the discomfort is bearable. But as we now know, a single fluctuation adding its strength to other fluctuations may become powerful enough to reorganise the whole system into a new pattern. Said in another way, the discomfort compounds into something that cannot be ignored.

Our frog is starting to sweat, and he realizes the pond never got so warm. He wants to go back to the pond and starts planning and preparing how to get there.

In the preparation phase, plans are made on how to solve the obstacles in the way of change. Support is identified, and we list skills needed to make the change. Initial small steps are carried out as a tester to see if the plan and skills are adequate.

Then at some point, action is taken. Our frog jumps out of the boiling pot.

But he jumps right into the messy middle phase of the change process.

The messy middle phase

The messy middle phase is sometimes referred to as the "rollercoaster of change." There are ups and downs and turns and circling back. Our frog must now navigate his escape out of the kitchen. There are obstacles like chairs, cats, human feet and brooms. And he isn't sure where the pond is; he just knows it is not in this kitchen.

Luckily for us, there is research on the experience of this transition. Based on the great work done by Kübler-Ross, who worked on how people deal with loss, the messy middle flows through similar phases. I found it helps to realize that in a change process, we are mourning the loss of the familiar "old way" that has served us well and to which we have become accustomed. An attitude of gratefulness towards the old way can help become change-fit. It played its role in the previous reality, but we are now entering a new reality that we must navigate.

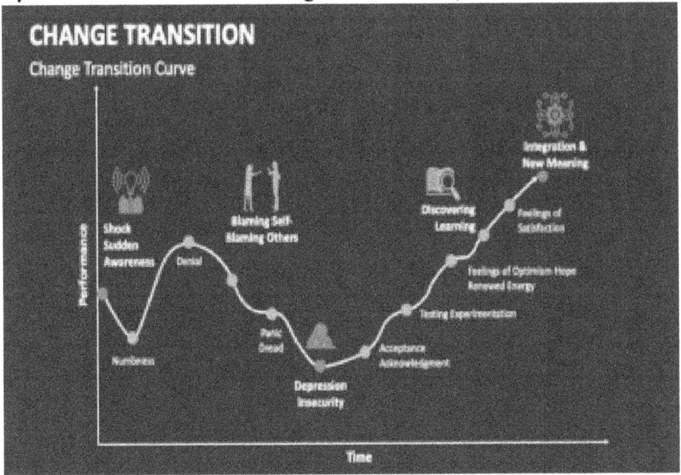

The rollercoaster starts with a shock or a sudden awareness. Our frog realizes he is going to become a meal for someone. Then follows a numbness that flows over into denial. We cannot believe this is happening to us. While we are numb and in denial, the rollercoaster has been chucking up a steep incline. As it makes its turn and shoots down, people typically start blaming themselves or others. If I did this or if you did that, we would not have been in this free fall. This bargaining or negotiating with whoever is useless as change is happening anyway. As the rollercoaster keeps on falling, panic and dread kick in as no solutions are obvious. This is when we hit rock bottom. The rollercoaster flattens out at the end of the slide down and we go into a depression and sense of insecurity.

But this is also the turning point. Acceptance and acknowledgement take place when embracing the new reality as being better than the old one. Our frog, hiding under a cupboard, sees the pond through the open back door.

The new beginnings

Because we have accepted the new reality, we start to experiment with what it could be like to live in this changed way. When the experiments succeed, we feel optimistic about what can be, and hope starts to inflame our hearts. There is renewed energy and feelings of satisfaction when we learn new things and as the rollercoaster stops at our destination, we have integrated the new reality as meaningful and right for us. Our frog jumps into the same old pond, but our frog has changed. It is stronger, more experienced and wiser. And, therefore, the pond is no longer the same pond.

Our story does not end here. Part of the change process is the maintenance of the new behaviour. For we now know that nothing lasts forever. Often, especially under a time of stress, relapse to the old way can happen.

Our frog in the pond must remember that a net sweeping through the water is not something to play with. Even if there is food in it.

Maintaining the new way includes planned follow-up support, reinforcing internal rewards and having a plan to cope with a relapse.

First, a quick word on *relapse*. Expect it.

Knowing that it will happen provides us with the opportunity to prepare for it and when it does happen, to be kind to ourselves while it happens. Positive support during the process of making mistakes is miles more efficient than stern criticism. Especially in the long run. From a mindset of "it-is-okay-you-did-your-best-up-to-now-let's-try-again" it is easier to learn from a mistake and be better equipped for the next round.

The relapse is just something to experience and work through. Take a moment, breathe deeply and start again. You will notice that as you become fitter, the relapses are shallower and shorter. Keep on keeping on.

One sure way to maintain the new way of being is to focus on habit formation. As Aristotle said, we are what we repeatedly do. Excellence therefore is a habit, not an event (paraphrased).

A *habit* is an action that is repeated regularly, sometimes without conscious awareness and tends to occur subconsciously. It is a settled tendency or usual manner of behaviour that has become nearly or completely involuntary.[xxx] Habits are formed through repeated actions and can be triggered by specific cues or contexts, leading to automatic behaviour.

Habits and routines or rituals are similar in that they both involve repeated actions, but they differ in several ways. A *routine* is a pattern of tasks that you consciously do repetitively, while a habit is an action that happens unconsciously. Routines require deliberate practice and effort, whereas habits are automatic and triggered by a particular cue.

Skipping a routine doesn't feel bad and can be easily skipped without proper forethought, while breaking a habit can feel uncomfortable. Additionally, habits are formed through associative learning, positive reinforcement and the role of context, while routines are created through deliberate choices. With enough time, routines can turn into habits, but not every routine can become a habit. Understanding the difference between habits and routines or rituals is important because it can help individuals create plans for lasting change.

We can learn a lot from James Clear when he talks about the paradox of change. He says, "Of course, change is possible, but it is only "*sustainable*" within a fairly narrow window. When an athlete trains too hard, she ends up sick or injured. When a company changes course too quickly, the culture breaks down and employees get burnt out. When a leader pushes his personal agenda to the extreme, the nation riots and the people re-establish the balance of power. Living systems do not like extreme conditions."[xxxi]

Consider the following quote from systems expert Peter Senge. "Virtually all natural systems, from ecosystems to animals to organisations, have intrinsically optimal rates of growth. The optimal rate is far less than the fastest possible growth. When growth becomes excessive – as it does in cancer – the system itself will seek to compensate by slowing down; perhaps putting the organisation's survival at risk in the process."

By contrast, when you accumulate small wins and focus on 1% improvements, you nudge equilibrium forward. It is like building muscle. If the weight is too light, your muscles will atrophy. If the weight is too heavy, you'll end up injured. But if the weight is just a touch beyond your normal weight, then your muscles will adapt to the new stimulus and equilibrium will take a small step forward.

It's like the Goldilocks story. This change is too big, this change is too small, this change is just right.

For change to last, we must work with the fundamental forces in our lives, not against them. Nearly everything that makes up your daily life has an equilibrium – a natural set point, a normal pace, a typical rhythm. If we reach too far beyond this equilibrium, we will find ourselves being yanked back to the baseline.

Thus, the best way to achieve a new level of equilibrium is not with radical change, but through small wins each day.

This is the great paradox of behaviour change. If you try to change your life all at once, you will quickly find yourself pulled back into the same patterns as before. But if you merely focus on changing your normal day, you will find your life changes naturally as a side effect. Small moment-by-moment choices lead to big changes. It's like an alcoholic saying no to one sip at a time.

Let us have a look at some of these daily habits that make a significant difference in dealing with change. We start with three foundation stones that are always present and then we move on to mental flexibility.

Foundation stones

Being change-fit starts with your body. All change impacts our body and when our body is healthy, we are better equipped to deal with change. So, let's look at three core healthy lifestyle building blocks. Sleep, diet and movement. The most underestimated foundation stone is sleep.

Sleep

Sleep plays a crucial role in building resilience. Adequate sleep can help you take on life's stresses when they inevitably happen.

During sleep, your brain processes each day's events, forming memories and discarding any unnecessary information that may otherwise clutter your mind. Good sleep is vital for your brain to function properly, and it helps you keep a better handle on your emotions and impulses. During sleep, the brain strengthens emotionally charged memories, which can help individuals better cope with stressors in the future.

Sleep and resilience share similar neuronal networks and crucial brain hubs, and sleep loss and loss of resilience share similar behavioural consequences. Consistently poor sleep can affect resilience in several ways, including creating emotional imbalance, lack of empathy, poor impulse control, negativity bias and lack of creativity. Trauma of all kinds may impact how well you sleep, regardless of how big or seemingly small the trauma feels.

Healthy sleeping habits, also known as sleep hygiene, can help you establish a consistent sleep pattern and improve the quality of your sleep. Here are some tips for better sleep. I find these help me get to sleep.

Things to do:

- Keep a consistent sleep schedule by going to bed and waking up at the same time. Ensure you get at least 7-8 hours of sleep by going to bed early enough that allows for this.

- Establish a relaxing bedtime routine. This can include activities like reading, taking a warm bath, or practising relaxation techniques.

- Make your bedroom quiet and relaxing. Keep the room at a comfortable, cool temperature and minimize exposure to bright light.

- Create a sleep-conducive environment. This includes using blackout curtains, earplugs, and a white noise machine if needed.

Things to avoid:

- Don't go to bed unless you're sleepy: If you don't fall asleep after 20 minutes, get out of bed and do a quiet activity without a lot of light exposure.

- Avoid using your bed for activities like working or watching TV, as this can create associations that make it harder to fall asleep. Use your bed only for rest, sleep and sex.

- Limit exposure to bright light in the evenings. Turn off electronic devices at least 30 minutes before bedtime.

- Avoid large meals, caffeine and alcohol before bedtime. These can disrupt your sleep.

Diet

Diet can influence resilience in several ways. Research has shown that a healthy diet is associated with greater resilience. For example, a study found that greater diet diversity is crucial in maintaining and improving cognitive function as it relates to resilience in older adults. Another study revealed that resilience was associated with an overall better diet quality, including greater intakes of seafood and whole-grain foods, and lower intakes of ultra-processed foods and sugary products. Additionally, nutritional fitness, which includes a healthy diet, contributes to resilience by helping individuals maintain a healthy weight and protects against diet-related diseases.

I am not a dietician, but I do know you need to eat more greens than proteins, and more proteins than carbs. I suggest you invest in sorting out your diet. It is the fuel that helps you deal with life's challenges. Anyway, the energy that comes from eating healthy is abundant.

Movement

Movement, particularly physical exercise, plays a significant role in promoting resilience. Exercise has been shown to have a positive impact on resilience, as it can protect against the effects of stressful events and prevent or minimize neurological diseases.

Some of the ways that movement influences our resilience include:

- Exercise can influence neurodevelopment and shape our adult brains to react to life's challenges.

- Exercise has been shown to increase galanin levels – a brain chemical associated with mental health – which can help individuals cope better with stress and boost their resilience.
- Exercise has profound effects on brain function and neurochemistry, promoting our general brain health.
- Movement, such as dance, can create more elasticity in our bodies, leading to elasticity of the mind and increased emotional resilience.

- Paying attention to your movement and body awareness can help you become more present and resilient, especially during stressful times.

Physical exercise does not have to be a big issue. Walking for 30 minutes, three times a week is sufficient. Doing stretches at home helps a ton. Going to dances is fun. You move your body and there is social interaction. Join a club like Walk for Life or Parkrun or join a gym. Go swimming if you are near the beach or pool. The point is to move and have fun while you do it.

With these foundation stones in place, let's explore some other practices that make us more resilient.

Flexibility of mind

Flexibility is one of the most underestimated disciplines to master. As physical flexibility helps so does mental flexibility. Especially when it comes to resilience.

In Chapters 1 and 2 we covered how to change your mind by making sure the story you tell yourself serves you well.

In Chapter 3 we covered the essential role of positive relationships. Here's another tip. The adage "Don't put all your eggs in one basket" applies here as well. You can also think of being flexible in your relationships. Make a point of building relationships with people who are not from your background, your culture, or your school of thought. Not only do you widen and enrich your perspective, but you also expand your safety net for when things change. We do not know where the solutions to our life's challenges will come from. Also, remember to have a friend is to be a friend.

One last thing to highlight in dealing with change is to be aware that relapses often happen because we do not know the difference between stress and anxiety.

In his book *Thriving with Anxiety,* Dr David Romarin explains that anxiety and fear are essentially the same, sharing the same brain circuitry and physiological responses associated with the fight or flight system.[xxxii] The key difference lies in the absence of an actual threat during anxiety, while fear is a response to a real danger. He further distinguishes between stress and anxiety, highlighting that stress results from an imbalance between demands and resources, while anxiety is a fear response triggered by perceived threats. He suggests that anxiety can be beneficial, prompting self-awareness and the need for recalibration in stressful situations.

In an interview with Brett McKay, he suggests that our desire for control, despite the limited control we do have, contributes to increased anxiety in modern life. Rosmarin emphasizes the importance of acknowledging discomfort as a natural part of being human and building emotional resilience.

The conversation also touches on managing stress through practices such as adequate sleep and regular exercise.

The point of this last piece of information is to bring home the truth the Stoics shared with us when we started our conversation. Change is the only constant, and it is futile to resist it. Resistance creates anxiety and anxiety depletes our change-fitness capacity. So go with the flow but keep your eyes wide open. Life is a joyride, regardless of its ups and downs.

And about change, if you are holding onto the past with two clenched hands, you have no hands to stretch out toward the future.

Conclusion

I have been thinking about Liam again. Remember, the young man we met at the start of this book? He lost his father, mended the fishing boat, and returned to the sea. Through his actions, he inspired the village to stand up again after the devastating storm.

So many of the elements we have covered link to that story.

Liam needed to believe in himself to start again. He needed to change the story about the sea as a dangerous place to the sea as a place that takes but gives more. He celebrated his strengths when he mended the fishing boat and made peace with his past as he returned to the sea.

He could only take these actions because he believed in his ability to choose and act. He lived in the creator quadrant of autonomy and initiated actions that were inside his sphere of influence.

He built positive relationships with the rest of the villagers as their criticisms changed to appreciation. He lived his values of taking care of his family and sharing the abundance of the sea harvest.

And I am sure he needed to communicate effectively to share his reasons for starting again as he accepted the heartache of the changed situation and started fishing again.

This reminds me of Rudyard Kipling's poem "IF":

If you can keep your head when all about you
Are losing theirs and blaming it on you,
If you can trust yourself when all men doubt you,
But make allowance for their doubting too;
If you can wait and not be tired by waiting,
Or being lied about, don't deal in lies,
Or being hated, don't give way to hating,
And yet don't look too good, nor talk too wise:
If you can dream – and not make dreams your master;
If you can think – and not make thoughts your aim;
If you can meet with Triumph and Disaster

And treat those two impostors just the same;
If you can bear to hear the truth you've spoken
Twisted by knaves to make a trap for fools,
Or watch the things you gave your life to, broken,
And stoop and build 'em up with worn-out tools:
If you can make one heap of all your winnings
And risk it on one turn of pitch-and-toss,
And lose, and start again at your beginnings
And never breathe a word about your loss;
If you can force your heart and nerve and sinew
To serve your turn long after they are gone,
And so hold on when there is nothing in you
Except the Will which says to them: 'Hold on!'
If you can talk with crowds and keep your virtue,
Or walk with Kings – nor lose the common touch,
If neither foes nor loving friends can hurt you,
If all men count with you, but none too much;
If you can fill the unforgiving minute
With sixty seconds' worth of distance run,
Yours is the Earth and everything that's in it,

And – which is more – you'll be ~~a Man, my son~~ [resilient, my friend]![2]
(Rudyard Kipling)

More About...

The Author

Herman Veitch holds a Master's degree in psychology with a focus on positive psychology. With over 20 years of experience in business, leadership, and life coaching, he currently lectures in knowledge management. This is his second book and uses the research done for his master's degree as a foundation for Getting Up Again.

Herman has exemplified resilience through significant life changes, including switching careers twice, living in six different countries, and overcoming the loss of loved ones. His extensive background and personal journey provide a rich foundation for the insights and strategies shared in his book.

The Accompanying Course

The eLearning course that accompanies this book can be found at http://hermanveitch.com/e-learning-projects/resilience-and-empowerment-transform-your-life-today/

This course focuses on practical exercises to implement the habits we discussed in this book. After doing the course, you will be able to:

- Have a positive attitude towards yourself -observe, categorize, and change your mental models and biases.
- Celebrate your diversity - understand and name your major personality dimensions as well as celebrate your uniqueness.
- Feel good about your past - recognise the major themes in your life story and rewrite your story in a constructive way
- Be the creator of your life - observe, categorize, and change your mental models regarding their agency and autonomy.
- Be value-driven - identify both your core values and actions that reflect these values.
- Have positive relationships - understand why positive relationships are important and identify types and phases in relationships. Then go beyond the basics of relationships - identify and set interpersonal boundaries as well as identify and avoid common relationship pitfalls.
- Effectively communicate - understand the communication process and be able to communicate whole messages.

- Be change fit - understand the change process, identify the stages of change and be prepared for upcoming change events.

Use this code to get a 10% discount on the course fee: FB2C10

The First Book

Herman's first book, *"Thinking About Thinking, An Introduction to Observing Your Own Mind,"* is a summary of the lessons learned after years of coaching. One reader said it is like having a personal coaching conversation in a book.

You can find the book on:

- Draft2Digital - https://books2read.com/b/4XYKK5

• • • •

---

[1]Stoicism, or Stoic philosophy, is a philosophy of personal ethics and a methodology for seeking practical wisdom. A key principle of the ancient Stoics was the belief that we don't react to events; we react to our judgements about them, and the judgements are up to us. They also advised that we should not worry about things beyond our control as everything in life can be divided into two categories – things that are up to us and things that are not. https://whatisstoicism.com/what-is-stoicism/

[2]Author taking liberty – please forgive him.

---

[i]Story co-created with ChatGPT.

[ii] The Resilience Factor: 7 Keys to Finding Your Inner Strength and Overcoming Life's Hurdles. Karen Reivich, Andrew Shatte, Ph.D. 2003

[iii] Ryff, C. D. & Keyes, C. L. M. (1995). The Structure of Psychological Wellbeing Revisited. *Journal of Personality and Social Psychology, 69(4),* 719-727.

[iv] https://www.marcandangel.com/2018/08/12/7-short-stories-that-will-change-your-attitude-and-spare-some-pain/

[v] Radden, Jennifer (ed.), 'A Learned Helplessness Model of Depression: SELIGMAN', in Jennifer Radden (ed.), The Nature of Melancholy: From Aristotle to Kristeva (New York, 2002; online edn, Oxford Academic, 3 Oct. 2011), https://doi.org/10.1093/acprof:oso/9780195151657.003.0028, accessed 7 July 2024.

[vi] Ruiz, Don M. The Four Agreements: A Practical Guide to Personal Freedom. San Rafael, CA: Amber-Allen Publishing, 2017.

[vii] https://rupikaur.com/ and https://www.best-poems.net/rupi-kaur/poems.html

[viii] https://www.britannica.com/science/memory-psychology and https://en.wikipedia.org/wiki/Recall_(memory)

[ix] Tagore, Rabindranath, and Surendranath Tagore. My Reminiscences. New York, The Macmillan company, 1916. Pdf. https://www.loc.gov/item/44029314/

[x] https://lchc.ucsd.edu/mca/Paper/00_01/agency.htm

[xi] https://cyc-net.org/cyc-online/cyconline-feb2024-delano.html

[xii]Frankl, V. E. (1984). *Man's search for meaning: An introduction to logotherapy*. New York: Simon & Schuster.

[xiii]See article I have written for the ICF http://coachfederation.org/about/ article.cfm?ItemNumber=1993&_ga=1.63890858.482002650.138909677

[xiv] https://www.megselig.com/

[xv] https://bigclosetr.us/topshelf/fiction/19008/ oak-and-willow-fable

[xvi] https://brenebrown.com/videos/the-power-of-being-vulnerable-with-jonathan-fields-of-good-life-project/

[xvii] https://www.news-medical.net/health/ What-are-Mirror-Neurons.aspx

[xviii] https://positivepsychology.com/mirror-neurons/

[xix] https://imgflip.com/i/46ijav

[xx] https://cognitiontoday.com/psychology-of-memes-advanced-emotions-outsourced-thoughts-mental-health/

[xxi] https://www.butte.edu/departments/cas/tipsheets/ thinking/reasoning.html

[xxii] Sellars, John (2006). Stoicism. Acumen Publishing.

[xxiii] www.themarginalian.org

[xxiv]https://www.e-careers.com/connected/10-businesses-that-failed-to-adapt

[xxv] Prigogine, I., & Stengers, I. (2018). Order Out of Chaos: Man's New Dialogue with Nature. Verso. ISBN 9781786631008[1]

[xxvi]https://images.squarespace-cdn.com/content/
5d572421dafa5e000131e362/1591480132127-
X9L6EIAV4TQRZ0RSAESR/
PeriodDoublingBifurcation4.png?format=1500w&content-
type=image%2Fpng

[xxvii] https://www.britannica.com/event/womens-movement

[xxviii] https://galileotakesastandforoursolarsystem.weebly.com/
galileos-impact-on-society.html

[xxix] https://bse.berkeley.edu/bruce-fuller

[xxx] https://www.merriam-webster.com/dictionary/habit and
https://edugage.com/what-is-a-habit-definition-facts-guide/

[xxxi] https://jamesclear.com/behavior-change-paradox

[xxxii] David H. Rosmarin is an American psychologist who specializes in anxiety. He is an associate professor at Harvard Medical School[2] and the founder and director of the Center for Anxiety. He is the author of *Thriving with Anxiety: 9 Tools to Make Your Anxiety*

---

1. https://www.penguinrandomhouse.com/books/643445/order-out-of-chaos-by-ilya-prigogine-and-isabelle-stengers/

2. https://en.wikipedia.org/wiki/Harvard_Medical_School

Work for You[3] taken from https://www.artofmanliness.com/health-fitness/health/podcast-947-turn-your-anxiety-into-a-strength/

---

3.   https://www.google.com/

search?sca_esv=4fab3e46d17faa58&rlz=1C1CHBF_enZA1076ZA1076&sxsrf=ACQVn08kA

2y72S8LuFeSHzmPJHkGOPT_aA:1706437334926&q=Thriving+with+Anxiety:+9+Tools+

to+Make+Your+Anxiety+Work+for+You&si=AKbGX_rO4P19IF_yO85wYpkEaz-

W_oZWd5JUOOVnUVftf2aeoccHeEY66ZZNKTDaAD9SZklBAzbd6cqevj4ddmtodbWu43

3Gs2tnz8eID0HUfzlX7l5LMsXqQ1KYpInUR1rRS8zeNT9blcu0uXvJ9Wtcps5Xc42WjAfac

DjPoMXh-XlfJCzFwHhDR9T-2criUkvLy0Wrqdp5vJ0_t7-

URWZKqdH8v9Uz4xOXTMVKJez-v2e3JmPbVGxpNXI2Tt-

r44XXAmib93bzJjVSscRngRCPJmh5lz6Wag%3D%3D&sa=X&ved=2ahUKEwipjbO57v-

DAxVaVUEAHUT_Ap8QmxMoAHoECBYQAg

Don't miss out!

Visit the website below and you can sign up to receive emails whenever Herman Veitch publishes a new book. There's no charge and no obligation.

https://books2read.com/r/B-A-HPCDB-DRCLD

Connecting independent readers to independent writers.